Designs of Darkness
in Contemporary American Fiction

PENN STUDIES IN CONTEMPORARY AMERICAN FICTION

A Series Edited by Emory Elliott, University of California at Riverside

A complete listing of the books in this series appears at the back of this volume

Designs of Darkness
in Contemporary American
Fiction

ARTHUR M. SALTZMAN

upp

University of Pennsylvania Press / PHILADELPHIA

Library of Congress Cataloging-in-Publication Data

Saltzman, Arthur M. (Arthur Michael), 1953–
    Designs of darkness in contemporary American fiction / Arthur M.
Saltzman.
      p.   cm. — (Penn studies in contemporary American fiction)
    Includes bibliographical references and index.
    ISBN 0-8122-3051-5
    1. American fiction—20th century—History and criticism.
2. Light and darkness in literature.   I. Title.   II. Series.
    PS374.L47S25   1990
    813'.509—dc20   90-12706
                                                  CIP

For Marla
For her light

Contents

Acknowledgments

The following publishers and authors of copyrighted works have generously granted permission to use quotations that exceed Fair Use standards:

From *How German Is It*, by Walter Abish. Copyright © 1979, 1980 by Walter Abish. Reprinted by permission of New Directions Publishing Corporation.

From *The American Novel and the Way We Live Now*, by John Aldridge. Copyright © 1983 by Oxford University Press. Reprinted by permission of Oxford University Press.

From "The Balloon," by Donald Barthelme, first published in *The New Yorker*, April 13, 1966. Copyright © 1966 by Donald Barthelme. Reprinted by permission of International Creative Management, Inc.

From "Bone Bubbles," by Donald Barthelme, first published in *The Paris Review*. Copyright © 1970 by Donald Barthelme. Reprinted by permission of International Creative Management, Inc.

From "The Glass Mountain," by Donald Barthelme, in *Sixty Stories* (1982). Copyright © 1970 by Donald Barthelme. Reprinted by permission of International Creative Management, Inc.

From *Diminishing Fictions: Essays on the Modern American Novel and Its Critics*, by Bruce Bawer. Copyright © 1988 by Graywolf Press. Reprinted by permission of Graywolf Press.

From *Fizzles*, by Samuel Beckett. Copyright © 1976 by Grove Press, Inc. Reprinted by permission of Grove Press, Inc.

From *Labyrinths*, by Jorge Luis Borges. Copyright © 1962, 1964 by New Directions Publishing Corporation. Reprinted by permission of New Directions Publishing Corporation.

From *I and Thou*, by Martin Buber, trans. Walter Kaufmann. Translation copyright © 1970 by Charles Scribner's Sons. Reprinted by permission of Charles Scribner's Sons, an imprint of Macmillan Publishing Company.

From *Humanities in America: A Report to the President, the Congress, and the American People*, by Lynne V. Cheney. Copyright © 1988 by Na-

From *Willie Masters' Lonesome Wife,* by William H. Gass. Copyright © 1968 by William H. Gass. Reprinted by permission of the author.

From *Cosmos,* by Witold Gombrowicz, excerpted in *Fiction of the Absurd: Pratfalls in the Void,* ed. Dick Penner. Copyright © 1980 by Grove Press, Inc. Reprinted by permission of Grove Press, Inc.

From "The Aura of a New Man," by Ihab Hassan, in *Salmagundi* 67 (1985), 165–66. Copyright © by *Salmagundi.* Reprinted by permission of *Salmagundi.*

From *Whistlejacket,* by John Hawkes. Copyright © 1988 by John Hawkes. Reprinted by permission of Weidenfeld & Nicolson, New York, a division of the Wheatland Corporation.

From *I Am a Memory Come Alive,* by Franz Kafka, trans. Nahum N. Glatzer. Copyright © 1974 by Schocken Books, published by Pantheon Books, a division of Random House, Inc. Reprinted by permission of Random House, Inc.

From *The Exagggerations of Peter Prince,* by Steve Katz. Copyright © 1970 by Henry Holt and Company, Inc. Reprinted by permission of Henry Holt and Company, Inc.

From *Moving Parts,* by Steve Katz. Copyright © 1977 by the Fiction Collective. Reprinted by permission of the Fiction Collective.

From *Weir and Pouce,* by Steve Katz. Copyright © 1984 by Steve Katz. Reprinted by permission of Sun & Moon Press.

From *Being There,* by Jerzy Kosinski. Copyright © 1970 by Harcourt Brace Jovanovich, Inc. Reprinted by permission of Harcourt Brace Jovanovich, Inc.

From "The Writer as Independent Witness," by Paul Levine, in *E. L. Doctorow: Essays and Conversations,* ed. Richard Trenner. Copyright © 1983 by Ontario Review Press. Reprinted by permission of Ontario Review Press.

From *Moby-Dick,* by Herman Melville, ed. Harrison Hayford and Hershel Parker. Copyright © 1967 by W. W. Norton & Co., Inc. Reprinted by permission of W. W. Norton & Co., Inc.

From *The Collected Poems of Howard Nemerov,* by Howard Nemerov. Copyright © 1977 by Howard Nemerov. Reprinted by permission of the author.

From *At Swim-Two-Birds,* by Flann O'Brien. Copyright © 1976 by Walker and Company. Reprinted by permission of Walker and Company.

From *Passionate Doubts: Designs of Interpretation in Contemporary Ameri-*

can Fiction, by Patrick O'Donnell. Copyright © 1986 by University of Iowa Press. Reprinted by permission of University of Iowa Press.

From *The Renewal of Literature: Emersonian Reflections,* by Richard Poirier. Copyright © 1987 by Alfred A. Knopf, Inc. Reprinted by permission of Alfred A. Knopf, Inc.

From *Malcolm,* by James Purdy. Copyright © 1959 by James Purdy. Reprinted by permission of the author.

From *The Crying of Lot 49,* by Thomas Pynchon. Copyright © 1965, 1966 by Thomas Pynchon. Reprinted by permission of Harper & Row, Publishers, Inc.

From "Walter Abish's *How German Is It:* Language and the Crisis of Human Behavior," by Dieter Saalman, in *Critique* 26.2 (1985), 117. Copyright © 1985 by Heldref Publications. Reprinted by permission of the Helen Dwight Reid Educational Foundation.

From "Epiphany and Its Discontents," by Arthur M. Saltzman, in *Journal of Modern Literature,* 15.4 (Spring 1990). Copyright © 1990 by Temple University Press. Reprinted by permission of Temple University Press.

From "The Stylistic Energy of E. L. Doctorow," by Arthur M. Saltzman. Copyright © 1983 by Ontario Review Press. Reprinted by permission of Ontario Review Press.

From *Styles of Radical Will,* by Susan Sontag. Copyright © 1969 by Farrar, Straus & Giroux, Inc. Reprinted by permission of Farrar, Straus & Giroux, Inc.

From *Odd Number,* by Gilbert Sorrentino. Copyright © 1985 by Gilbert Sorrentino. Reprinted by permission of North Point Press.

From "The Detective and the Boundary," by William V. Spanos, in *Boundary 2* 2 (Fall 1972), 149–50, 152. Copyright © 1972 by *Boundary 2.* Reprinted by permission of *Boundary 2* and the author.

From *The Collected Poems of Wallace Stevens,* by Wallace Stevens. Copyright © 1954 by Alfred A. Knopf, Inc. Reprinted by permission of Alfred A. Knopf, Inc.

From *Mr. and Mrs. Baby and Other Stories,* by Mark Strand. Copyright © 1985 by Mark Strand. Reprinted by permission of the Robert Cornfield Literary Agency and the author.

From *Reasons for Moving,* by Mark Strand. Copyright © 1968 by Mark Strand. Reprinted by permission of the Robert Cornfield Literary Agency and the author.

From *Long Talking Bad Condition Blues,* by Ronald Sukenick. Copyright

Chapter 1

Introduction: A De-Meaning Poetics

"Where is the figure in the carpet? Or is it just . . . carpet?"
—from *Snow White*, by Donald Barthelme

In his commencement oration at Harvard in 1837, Henry David Thoreau described this world as "more wonderful than convenient,"[1] but it was not until recently that American fiction began to address this prospect with regularity. Partly as a result of feeling reproached by the world, the novel redirects its attentions to itself, as is most evident in the self-consultive, self-scavenging concerns of metafiction as it fingers its own linguistic privates.

Our secular perplexity has paradoxically been met by the arrival of literary studies at a point of remarkable and unprecedented sophistication. The adversarial energies of Modernism have so effectively transformed our sensibilities that the revolutionary has become the orthodox; the exemplary texts of High Modernism are today as entrenched and canonical as the prior Establishment had been. So it seems that literary and political histories share evolutionary characteristics; insurgent movements, led by legitimating manifestos and cries of freedom, storm the castle only to grow into hoary standards themselves some day. Whom the gods would subdue they first anthologize.

The uneasy relationship between Postmodernism and its Modernist legacy is, of course, a long-standing definitional issue among numerous critics who debate whether the distance between them is sufficient to warrant separate coinages.[2] Like an obstreperous child who nevertheless keeps looking back to a parent for encouragement and validation, Postmodern Fiction (whose aliases include Surfiction, Postrealist Fiction, Anti-Fiction, and New Fiction) is a field that appears to be endlessly vulnerable to gatecrashing neologists. My own purposes in this study, however, have only tangentially to do with determining the rank of current fiction. Nor do I propose to enlist in the argument over whether metafictional fireworks still amaze or have by now fallen to earth as ash.

Instead, I would like to focus on what I believe to be the central cause of critical defensiveness and accusations of treachery against contemporary fiction: its pronounced tendency to let ambiguities blossom far beyond our capacities to stabilize, summarize, or restore them to sense. The old rules of the game—anxious grasping after Truth is rewarded by a more or less reliably "composed" product, and readerly resolve by narrative resolution—cannot be confidently applied. Literature comes out of the answerless, our authors now seem to tell us, and we touch the reminders shut in books, which are never so clever as calendars or so certain as the railroad timetables Kafka's Gregor Samsa used to peruse for the pleasure of firmness.

There is a cultish quality to proponents of the view that interpretation may not trespass with impunity upon what Samuel Beckett (whose example serves throughout this study) has termed "the fixity of mystery." (To be sure, many of the most vociferous among them, such as Jonathan Baumbach, Raymond Federman, Gilbert Sorrentino, and Ronald Sukenick, are paving the way for their own disorienting prose styles.) They challenge the conventions of access and accommodation that constitute the usual contracts drawn up among author, book, and audience, daring us to adapt ourselves to fiction that purports to escape subjection to preexistent reality and launch competitive alternatives. Raymond Federman's notorious extremism on the subject is especially revealing, for the tone of his predictions regarding the unprecedented influx of ambiguity into our stories is not desolate but celebratory; he eagerly anticipates fiction that "will be seemingly devoid of any meaning . . . deliberately illogical, irrational, unrealistic, non sequitur, and incoherent."[3] Not even the oppositional experiments of the Modernists dispelled the belief that Meaning crouched in the bushes to be beaten out by teachers and be put to tests and that revelations hovered over each fiction, ready to descend like gulls to a feeding. On the contrary, contemporary fiction so respects—even advocates—the resistance of experience (of world and word alike) to decipherability that interpretation may no longer be seen as the vanquishment of fiction but as its inevitable extension.

Renowned, too, are those gruff arbiters of literary culture for whom such protests and radical displacements mask a failure of moral rectitude, artistic talent, or individual nerve. John Gardner, in his much-debated book *On Moral Fiction*, bemoans the wholesale abandonment of "models of virtue" for texture alone.[4] In Gardner's estimation, contemporary fiction is characterized by a fatal settlement for the trivial:

For the most part our artists do not struggle—as artists have traditionally struggled—toward a vision of how things ought to be or what has gone wrong; they do not provide us with the flicker of lightning that shows us where we are. Either they pointlessly waste our time, saying and doing nothing, or they celebrate ugliness and futility, scoffing at good. (16)

What accomplishments today's authors do make, Gardner complains, are primarily technical, and they "have little to do with the age-old search for understanding and affirmation" (71). That they may in fact be aspects of perpetuating that search—indeed, that they may be among the results of that search—Gardner does not allow. He rests his case with formulaic self-assurance on the matter: "The difference between what merits being called classical prose and the prose of most of our writers is a matter of confidence, of belief" (97). Clearly, the contours of confidence and belief are clear enough to Gardner himself, and the tone of his appraisal is as much one of bewilderment as it is one of dismay at the rudderless preoccupations of so many of his colleagues.

In keeping with Gardner (whose own novels he spares from assault), John Aldridge suggests that contemporary fiction is suffering the consequences of its unwillingness to undertake the proper agenda of reflecting public consciousness and our need for examples of transcendence. Because writers seem incapable of authentically engaging the complexities of their real-world environment, "the self becomes its own environment and sole source of authenticity, while all else becomes abstract and alien."[5] Faddish nihilism excuses writers from devising superior perspectives; "Verisimilitude and sanity have been nullified," while novelistic activity "becomes inexplicably arbitrary and unjudgeable because the fiction itself stands as a metaphor of derangement that is seemingly without provocation and beyond measurement" (140). Aldridge assails many of the same names as Gardner: Barth, Coover, Doctorow, Heller, Mailer, and Pynchon are targets common to both, while Elkin, Gass, Hawkes, Purdy, and Sukenick are among several others who appear on one blacklist or the other. Selling out "both the ideal and the reality of individual self-discovery and transcendence as central thematic preoccupations" does not lead them to a corrective vision but to an eschewal of visionary alternatives altogether. Entrapment "in a demythologized and therefore demoralized present" is cheap pessimism in Aldridge's eyes. It does not offer instruction, only feeble confirmation of our sense that we are eternally out of our depth (10).

Likewise, Bruce Bawer longs for the titanic struggles of Dreiser, Hemingway, Faulkner, and Fitzgerald, for whose protagonists despair, even though seldom relieved, was deeply dimensioned and more richly earned. (It is intriguing to discover the Modernists, who had once been viewed as excessively nihilistic, now being looked back upon with such wistfulness!) Since World War II, says Bawer:

> there has generally been more compulsive gloom and doom than there has been forceful opposition to it. . . . [I]n one book after another, the major novelists of our day have, intentionally or not, allowed their relentless negativism to work against the best interest of the form itself; wittingly or unwittingly, they have renounced the vitality, the abundance, and the breadth of artistry that for more than two centuries have consistently distinguished the great novels of the world.[6]

Immediately Bawer acknowledges that these postwar novelists may feel that, given the chaotic, hostile nature of contemporary reality, they "have no choice" when it comes to style and argument; hence, he does grant them, albeit grudgingly, the possibility of integrity. But there is no mistaking his allegiance to Gardner and Aldridge in calling for a resumption of an enlarged manner and outlook by writers of fiction. It is when the world is most meaningless, these three concur, that art must mean most, and most clearly.

Donald Barthelme's "The Balloon" neatly anticipates such reactions to the impregnability of fictional realms by parodying the futility of conventional analytical gestures. Like a silent, seamless new moon, a massive balloon appears without warning or explanation over New York City. The indefinability of this "concrete particular, hanging there,"[7] because it can neither be ignored nor assimilated into "the grid of precise, rectangular pathways under our feet" (57), provokes a wide variety of reactions from the astonished population: hostility, anxiety, timorousness, exhilaration. As we might also expect, the critics rise to the occasion, delivering their sundry praises, petulances, and explications in its shadow. And with everyone casting his or her line at once, the result is a tangled mess. Some dismiss the balloon out of hand—"monstrous pourings," "*Quelle catastrophe!*"; others are cautious—"certain contrasts with darker portions," "large square corners"—or contemplative—"conservative eclecticism that has so far governed modern balloon design," "Has unity been sacrificed for a sprawling quality?" Some attest to its "inner joy" and "abnormal vigor," while still others are elliptical or just plain odd about it— "harp," "munching" (56–57).

As Barthelme's narrator admonishes, it is hazardous to accept any reading of the balloon, whose "deliberate lack of finish, enhanced by skillful installation" (as apt a description of Barthelme's own prose as we might hope to find, by the way) cajoles us into inferences and plausibilities but resists solutions (53–54). Only "cases involving the simplest, safest phenomena" (54), we are warned, can be subjected to universal formulations without causing dissent. But not all of the balloon's observers are defeated by the limitless challenge of the looming, blank surface. The balloon "offered the possibility, in its randomness, of mislocation of the self" to people mesmerized by the channels they had otherwise been resigned to before its arrival on the scene (57). Proximity brings warmth. The adventurous hang lanterns from it; a few scribble messages on the inviting underbelly; others secretly rendezvous under the cover it provides. Children make a game out of leaping onto its "pneumatic" skin where it draws closest to the city buildings, much the way people commute between earth and moon in Italo Calvino's fantasy "The Distance of the Moon,"[8] and couples even stroll through the creases. For those open to mystery, in other words, the balloon proves rather more liberating than obstructive or aggravating.

The catalytic, reorienting potential of the balloon is powerful enough to eclipse all previous thinking about balloons—that is, at least for the twenty-two days during which it is there. All attitudes have to contend with its presence and develop in terms of it; contact threatens "mislocation of the self" on the one hand, expansion of the self on the other. (Perhaps they are one and the same thing obscured by a trick of perspective or the headiness caused by "inflation.") To treat Barthelme's grand conceit as a claim for contemporary fiction, of course, is still to exhibit the same penchant for consoling, decodable symbols that "The Balloon" playfully indicts. Suffice it to say that Barthelme's siege against meaning is symptomatic of, depending on one's standards and the rigidity of his expectations, the enigmatic, disconcerting, enchanting nature of recent fiction.

I have arranged *Designs of Darkness in Contemporary American Fiction* so as to highlight several ways in which fiction traditionally conspires to promote a goal-oriented, teleologically certifiable vision of the work of art, from which vantage points I investigate how specific texts "trouble the harmonies." In each chapter I attempt to lay bare the devices of signification, or more aptly, to reveal the methods evident in so many contemporary novels to "de-mean" their own cunning constructions. "Epiphany and Its Discontents" dismantles the myth of revelational witchery in which spells of blinding or bitter clarity (exhibitions of significance strong enough to split stone) are exposed by contemporary authors as verbal mirages. "Deregulating Histories" looks at the promiscuity of fiction and history, which, deriving from and contaminated by the same urges and premises, are in the end indistinguishable and necessarily incomplete. Causality and determinism, those stiff twin compasses of explanation, are at last a broken conspiracy. (Empirical confidence may be associated with reconciling a checkbook, but never with reading a novel!)

In "De(in)forming the Plot," I examine how contemporary fiction employs characters who are not un-selfconscious but unself-conscious, aware of their fragile identities in narrative formulas of detection and quest only to sabotage their chain-linked logical operations. "Opacity, Resistance, and the Uncommunicative Text" shows how fiction's increasing attention to the fundamental arbitrariness and materiality of its "wordstuff" makes any foray into a book provisional and treacherous. By way of conclusion, "The End of Value?" considers and qualifies the belief in moral content and transmission as a priority when it comes to how and why we teach literature, as well as what literature we choose to teach. Far-ranging and disruptive as contemporary fiction's skepticism about traditional modes of meaning proves to be, still it foreshadows—it mandates—evolving strategies for accommodating our unflagging appetite for narrative.

I might summarize my motives by saying that I want to talk about the impact on fiction of taking Sir Philip Sidney's dictum that the poet "nothing affirms, and therefore never lies" quite literally. He instead only goes "freely ranging within the zodiac of his own wit,"[9] another phrase whose present-day applicability Sidney could not have envisioned. Rattling about within the vast, uncompromisable magnitude of human experience, hobbled by the same awareness of the artificial verbal medium that sustains them, contemporary authors are at once humbler and more rash than those ancestors preferred by the likes of Gardner, Aldridge, and Bawer. For even as they confess their limits, they achieve eloquence in confession; with meaning withheld and associations undermined by their own intrusive desires, they locate aesthetic faith, such as it can be, in the elegant perpetuation of process. Like Wallace Stevens's Crispin, contemporary American writers concede to the "insoluble lump" of the world, which had reportedly been "a turnip once so readily plucked," and "[concoct] doctrine from the rout."[10]

In trying to portray the variety and scope of responses to the disqualification of epiphanic faith, I have chosen representative works by several authors who dominate discussions of Postmodern fiction, which is to say, those whose works are frequently used to suggest the justifiability of speaking of a distinctive new period in American fiction. I also try to complement them with analyses of fiction by less familiar hands. Thus, in addition to such stalwarts of the critical wars as Walter Abish, John Barth, Donald Barthelme, Thomas Berger, Robert Coover, Don DeLillo, E. L. Doctorow, John Hawkes, Jerzy Kosinski, James Purdy, Gilbert Sorrentino, and Ronald Sukenick, I consider fictions by writers like Paul Auster, Kenneth Gangemi, Steve Katz, and Rudolph Wurlitzer, whose names are perhaps not as immediately recognized but whose contributions likewise help to indicate the "de-meaning" features I propose to emphasize. Although *Designs of Darkness in Contemporary American Fiction* may not win converts to its subjects among conservative critics, I hope that it will provide them, and others who are frustrated by the widespread renovation of the literary enterprise, with demonstrations of more rewarding access.

I am pleased to acknowledge those outlets in which earlier versions of portions of this book first appeared. Chapter Two was originally published in slightly altered form in *Journal of Modern Literature*. My analysis of *The Book of Daniel* began as part of my synthetic discussion of "The Stylistic Energy of E. L. Doctorow" in *E. L. Doctorow: Essays and Conversations,* edited by Richard Trenner. Finally, an abbreviated version of Chapter Five first appeared in *Publications of the Missouri Philological Association* under the title "Communication and Resistance: On Opaque Fictions." I am grateful for these opportunities to have exercised my ideas and for permission to reprint them here. I am also indebted to Morton Levitt, James Justus, Patrick O'Donnell, and Joel Brattin, all of whom read and offered comment on portions of this study. Finally, and as always, I would like to thank my wife, Marla, for her patience, support, and abiding love.

Chapter 2
Epiphany and Its Discontents

It's only considering the linguistic manifestation of a wish
that makes it appear that my wish prefigures the fulfillment.
—Because it's the wish that just that were the case.—It is in
language that wish and fulfillment meet.

Instead of "to know something" we might say "to keep a
piece of paper on which it is written."

When I talk about language (words, sentences, etc.) I must
speak the language of every day. Is this language somehow
too coarse and material for what we want to say? Then how
is another one to be constructed?—And how strange that we
should be able to do anything at all with the one we have!

How strange that one should be able to say that such and
such a state of affairs is inconceivable! If we regard thought
as essentially an accompaniment going with an expression,
the words in the statement that specify the inconceivable
state of affairs must be unaccompanied. So what sort of sense
is it to have? Unless it says these words are senseless. But it
isn't as it were their sense that is senseless; they are excluded
from our language like some arbitrary noise, and the reason
for their *explicit* exclusion can only be that *we are tempted* to
confuse them with a sentence of our language.

—from *Philosophical Grammar,* by Ludwig Wittgenstein

On the shore of the essential, vision's bright verge.

We are near the end of Robert Frost's "Design."[1] Our speaker has just
witnessed the remarkable fusion of a fat white spider, a white moth, and a
white heal-all into a single image, as though placed there for his benefit
and instruction. How else to explain the surprising whiteness of the
spider, the coincident whiteness of the moth in its grasp, and the odds-
defying hue of a plant whose blossoms are typically blue-violet? And what
unseen Destiny marked them for convergence? "What but design of
darkness to appall?" asks the poet (line 13). Surely this event (not to
mention the poet's fortuitous presence) is telling evidence against randomness in the universe; surely the "design of darkness" is "appalled"—

both "dismayed" and "made pale," as befits the literal metamorphosis of the elements of nature in this poem—by this triumph of purpose.

But the final line of the poem is a crucial disclaimer against the insight: "If design govern in a thing so small" (line 14). Does Providence guide such negligible affairs? Moreover, even if this *is* an example of superhuman design, it is a somber one, composed of "assorted characters of death and blight" (line 4). Perhaps *we* are the ones appalled by the design of darkness. No wonder the poet retreats from conviction! In Nietzsche's words, "We have art in order that we not be destroyed by the truth."[2] In fact, upon reflection, the only design we can be certain of is not nature's at all, but rather that of the poem itself—its philosophical execution, its stalwart sonnet form. Schemes of meter and rhyme are scheming indeed, as art assaults the world with the artist's resolve to humanize the environment.

Frost's poem precisely anticipates the qualified status of epiphany among the postmodernists, for whom "felt ultimacies"—the passages that so readily attract brackets and stars—are opportunities for deflation by metafictional techniques.[3] My focus, therefore, is upon the deflationary impact of the exposure of epiphany as being the design of literary custom or authorial intention.

The tradition that anti-epiphanic fiction debates or parodies is most extensively treated by Morris Beja in *Epiphany in the Modern Novel.* Early in this landmark study, Beja provides an operational definition of his key term: "a sudden spiritual manifestation, whether from some object, scene, event, or memorable phase of the mind—the manifestation being out of proportion to the significance or strictly logical relevance of whatever produces it."[4] Beja is quick to note that his definition makes provision for revelations that recall the significance of the past during present circumstances as well as for those that recover the past but only now appreciate its latent significance. In either case, literary epiphany is a frozen moment of rare access into the heart of things—an unexpected synthesis. However, Beja's definition does not differentiate between points of origin: whether the epiphany is a manifestation external to the imagination that is privileged to receive it, or whether it is a product of the imagination itself, is not determined. Perhaps this is because the effect of the epiphany is unaffected by this distinction; perhaps it is simply because the character who has the epiphany cannot tell to what degree he has created what he perceives, or indeed, because he does not wish to jeopardize the moment with such intellectual sacrilege.

It is my contention that the latter explanation—epiphanies are made, not born—provides a better bridge toward understanding the treatment of epiphany in postmodern fiction. Recalling Wallace Stevens's contention in "The Idea of Order at Key West" that "there was never a world for her/Except the one she sang and, singing, made,"[5] we can see how revelations are primarily linguistic rather than spiritual. Words do not commemorate the experience, they constitute it. Even if epiphany begins with enchantment, or a desire for enchantment, it is only authenticated through the process of articulation.

Let us return temporarily to a famous modern example of an epiphanic instant. It is proper that we turn to Joyce, to whom we are indebted for turning "epiphany" into a literary term. Stephen Dedalus is on the verge of an intuition of his artistic vocation:

—A day of dappled seaborne clouds.—

> The phrase and the day and the scene harmonised in a chord. Words. Was it their colours? He allowed them to glow and fade, hue after hue: sunrise gold, the russet and green of apple orchards, azure of waves, the grey fringed fleece of clouds. No, it was not their colours; it was the pause and balance of the period itself. Did he then love the rhythmic rise and fall of words better than their associations of legend and color? Or was it that, being as weak of sight as he was shy of mind, he drew less pleasure from the reflection of the glowing sensible world through the prism of a language many coloured and richly storied than from the contemplation of an inner world of individual emotions mirrored perfectly in a lucid supple periodic prose.[6]

Stephen Dedalus demonstrates a particularly lavish style throughout *A Portrait of the Artist,* as befits a young man trying to live up to the standards of a "rather florid imagination."[7] Accord arises from a chord that "harmonizes" the landscape. But it is also a style specifically devised to live up to the majesty Stephen needs this moment to represent; the container must be worthy of the jewel it stores. When in a later episode Stephen muses over the line "Darkness falls from the air," "A trembling joy, lambent as a faint light, played like a fairy host around him. But why? Her passage through the darkening air or the verse with its black vowels and its opening sound, rich and lutelike?"[8] If the quality of the insight is dependent upon the quality of the utterance, the epiphany itself becomes the initial test and product of Stephen's artistic virtuosity. The job of literary style is to retain the delicacy of the impression while ensuring its permanence. It is the passage, not the past, to which we return.

Postmodern fiction, because it does not traffic in the modernist presumption "that art can serve, in its own way, even the highest function which traditional religion purportedly serves,"9 more readily lays bare the artifice of epiphany. If epiphany is a focused, stabilized locus of meaning, contemporary reality, at least as it is inferred from recent fiction, is decentered, multivalent, unsystematic, even nonsensical. To use the terminology of Mas'ud Zavarzadeh in *The Mythopoeic Reality,* the totalizing novel, the integrated view of reality it propounds, and the prophetic status it bestows upon (or demands of) the author are hopelessly outdated.10 Epiphany is an anthropomorphic distortion, as could well be said of metaphor, analogy, or any of literature's ploys for rendering the world hospitable. As Alain Robbe-Grillet has extensively argued, our anxiety to provoke the world into conforming to a metaphysical system obliterates the world and replaces it with "the result of an intention."11 We lose the world in order to discover the comforts of feeling situated: "Drowned in the *depths* of things, man ultimately no longer even perceives them: his role is soon limited to experiencing, in their name, totally *humanized* impressions and desires."12 Postmodern fiction exposes the trick of holding a mirror up to our desires and calling them a true picture of reality, which is the illusion fiction has traditionally offered.

The paradox surrounding epiphany, then, is that it requires a fall into art, which, because art is a self-confessed sham among the postmodernists, undermines the lessons of epiphany by virtue of the artificial context from which it originates. After all, fiction's very name should put us on guard against its statements.

Another obstruction to epiphany that contemporary American fiction delights in exposing is the fact that language systems have their own organizational agenda. Coherence is prioritized, and its components include consequence (as opposed to mere sequence), causality, and destination, or climax.13 Fiction is inherently purposive; when an individual work of fiction stresses discontinuity and disharmony, it does so in part to satirize the conventions upon which the epiphanic tradition depends.

Fiction rewrites the world, shaping it to suit our longing, and postmodern fiction unveils the verbal essence and consequence of that longing, as well as of the revelations it summons. When, for example, William Gass celebrates Stanley Elkin's surging, excessive style, he locates epiphany firmly on the page: "*Vision* . . . is no visionary's word, no politician's promise, preacher's ploy. It is the unerring instinct of the verbal eye."14

Postmodern fiction ungirds those formidable conventions that suspend our disbelief, for only a wary reader, as purposefully self-conscious as the text he enters, will be an effective accomplice in the making of revelation.

As we turn in earnest to some exemplary postmodern fictions, we discover a persistent tension between the constitutive instinct we usually bring to our reading experience and the obstacles that prevent meaning from becoming established. Robert Coover is renowned for simultaneously calculating and dismantling his visions; fictional structures flower and fade with the speed of a magician's sleight-of-hand. In fact, fiction and magic are regularly identified with each other in his stories because they share the same properties: both are primarily entertainments; both require the indulgence of a reader/audience in order to be effective; both ordain rules that are appropriate solely to those individual activities; and both are transitory events. Solid gamesmanship, rather than priestly authority, underlies the fiction-maker's trade.

Epiphany seems so somber! Coover is a playful heretic when it comes to art's self-righteous presumption to Significance. His symbols no sooner sink in than they reveal their seams. Audacious metafictions all, his stories advertise themselves as stories, and sometimes they are barely *that*, as the story's reach does not always exceed its concept. Like Beckett's eloquent expressions of inexpressibility, Coover's fictions often complain of their own inertia. Coover holds open rehearsal for possible plots in "The Babysitter," or he junks the whole tired bag of tricks in "The Hat Act," making a story out of the futility of trying to convince anybody out there.

So Coover exchanges conviction for a confluence of potentialities. He seems to have taken his cue from Borges' story "The Garden of Forking Paths," which describes a brand of "exfoliating" fiction that anticipates Coover with precision: "In all fictional works, each time a man is confronted with several alternatives, he chooses one and eliminates the others; in the fictions of Ts'ui Pen, he chooses—simultaneously—all of them. *He creates,* in this way, diverse futures, diverse times which themselves also proliferate and fork."[15] As to the fate of epiphany, Coover is quite succinct when he says, "I am inclined to believe that portentous inscrutability may be the point of it all."[16]

In his Prologue to the seven briefest fictions in *Pricksongs and Descants,* Coover dedicates these efforts to Cervantes in the name of resuscitating fiction by restoring its original "aura of possibility." Coover proclaims and practices a new faith in fabulism as a means of returning us "to the creation of Beauty within the confines of cosmic or human necessity" (78). This creed quite readily turns the worshipper into an active designer: Beauty is rendered according to the dictates of "human necessity." We are being offered haystacks pre-stocked with needles. How can any insight transcend the author's conjuring? Epiphany is a transparent trick up Coover's sleeve.

"Panel Game" expresses Coover's skepticism by mocking our addiction to associative thinking, as though Truth lurked just beyond the next "like." The Moderator is the author getting his revenge on readers who prefer the dependable accommodations of realistic literature and on critics who pin their careers on ferreting out symbolic patterns and plucking from the pages the correct key to the castle. The audience's representative is a Bad Sport wrested from the grandstand and forced to participate in the fiction, which is a game of ambiguous rules and improbable conclusion. He is confronted with THE BIG QUESTION, and automatically, desperately, ransacks his imagination for clues:

> So think. Stickleback. Freshwater fish. Freshwater fish: green seaman. Seaman: semen. Yes, but green: raw? spoiled? vigorous? Stickle: stubble. Or maybe scruple. Back: Bach: Bacchus: baccate: berry. Raw berry? Strawberry? Maybe. Sticky berry in the raw? In the raw: bare. Bare berry: beriberi. Also bearberry, the dog rose, dogberry. Dogberry: the constable, yes, right, the constable in . . . what? *Comedy of Errors!* Yes! No. (80)

Void and plenum are equally frustrating: meaningless and meaning-laden universes are equally inhospitable to the player who has been weaned on decipherability. "'Muteness is mutinous and the mutable inscrutable!' cries the Moderator, warming to the moment now, riding on waves of grand hosannas. 'Inflexibly same the *the lex of the game!*'" (84). THE BIG QUESTION is but a play of words, and there is no answer, only plays on words. The beleaguered contestant is doomed from the start: first, because the game is fixed, and taking it seriously contradicts its nebulous terms; second, because the mind is simply not attuned to arbitrariness, and it therefore fastens on details as though they were clues to a puzzle and holds on for dear order. The Moderator mocks us, the audience scorns our feeble display, but we cannot disobey our inclinations.

William V. Spanos attributes this passion for continuity to "the rational or rather the positivistic structure of consciousness that views spatial and temporal phenomena in the world as 'problems' to be 'solved' . . . [and] obsessively attempts by coercion to fix and stabilize the elusive flux of existence from the vantage point of a final rational cause."[17] Empirical probings hide the motive of creating human dominion over the world's data; the "totalized" environment results from totalitarian control. The "detective" in us, to use Spanos's term, is ruthlessly premeditative. Extending this mode of consciousness to literature, we find that this "self-deceptive effort to evade the anxiety of contingent existence" correlates to so-called well-made plots whose endings are consoling solutions.[18] Closure provides a sense of adequacy in an atmosphere of confusion. It seems to confirm an abiding trust between self and world that is strong enough to withstand the petty disturbances that "interrupt" the fiction and delay closure's reign.[19] Loose ends are tied, fates parceled out, obscurities illuminated. Centripetal and integrated, these fictions are funneled toward their formal destinies like children toward proper exits during fire drill. And to the satisfaction of literary critics, closed texts legitimate interpretation—they *invite* it, until "the skin of the world is littered with our contentious artifice, lepered with the stigmata of human aggression and despair."[20]

Thus, Coover contrives fictions that resist domestication and preempt our management tactics; like the unwilling contestant in "Panel Game," we cannot reach any interpretive high ground. Replacing "the luminous silent stasis of esthetic pleasure"[21] are the hoots and catcalls of Coover's callous crowd. The victim of the insidious panel game recalls Beckett's Unnamable, who, in a climate of relentless indeterminacy, churns words without resolve in the vain hope that he might purchase approval, or release, from a pitiless Master.

"Panel Game" is less dire about these circumstances; "much ado about nothing" is hinted at as the missing answer, and our representative player is dispatched with a parting goose. "Panel Game" shows us that there is no turning back to an uncontaminated perception of reality. We are irretrievably post-lapsarian on the subject of systematizing. The Moderator knows we cannot help ourselves; we slip grids into every river and set metaphors like bear traps along our paths. Meanwhile, epiphany is a delusion: THE BIG QUESTION is a hollow black box. "Panel Game" strips and teases anyone who plays.

"Klee Dead" likewise pokes fun at the "disease of the western mind" (106) whose symptoms are a rage for order and documentation, impatience with gaps, inconsistencies, and digressions, and a predilection for cause-effect logic. Wilbur Klee is dead—by definition, by decree, by dint of the brute "given" that opens the story: "Klee, Wilbur Klee, dies. Is dead, rather. I know I know: too soon. It should come, after a package of hopefully ingenious preparations, at the end: and thus, gentle lector, Wilbur Klee is gathered to his fathers. But what's to be done? He's already gone" (104). Just as we prefer the news of a human death to be softened by euphemism, we wish to be prepared for the death of a fictional character, as though swathing the event in detail grants it tragic proportion, if not ultimate justification. But Coover cannot turn back from having pronounced sentence, as it were, on Wilbur Klee, for in fiction, word and deed are one.

How do we explain and digest a death? Our narrator turns his attention to Millicent Gee, who is not dead, immediately making her more profitable as a subject of study. Whether or not the information we receive about her illuminates the truncated story of Klee, or whether it is meant to do so, is unclear; Millie is an eccentric, solitary old lady, and an understanding of her could prove useful in uncovering Klee's motives for jumping off a building, but we are admonished against making rash connections. When Millie's son briefly enters the story, we are restrained: "To tell the truth, I wish I hadn't brought him up in the first place. Please forget I mentioned him, if you can. What's more, I'm not entirely sure why I told you about Millie. Certainly she can have nothing to do with Wilbur Klee" (106). Every association is a false lead. For that matter, the assumption that Klee's death is a suicide is dubious, given the fact that, as creator, keeper, and dispenser of fates, Coover "pushed" him. Still, we cannot abide meaninglessness; we are driven to adopt an attitude. Coover is willing to accommodate us in this way, so long as we do not forget that we have chosen an artificial convenience for the sake of getting on with it, nothing more: "As for the rest of it, if you wish to believe as I do that he took his own life, fine! It certainly will make it easier for me as we wind this up. But I won't be dogmatic about it" (107).

Coover's method in "The Babysitter" is to include all the possible narrative choices simultaneously; in "The Elevator," he retraces the same fictional ground—like an elevator, the story moves vertically instead of progressing horizontally—and presents his choices consecutively, as though parading fashions before us; in "Klee Dead," the impasses are so expressly foregrounded that the central story cannot get under way. Ironically, the very state of "disequilibrium, suspense, and general insufficiency" that occasions "narratability" in traditional fiction[22] has grown so intense as to threaten the development of the story at all. Not even the names of characters are safe from equivocation.

Because our penchant for explanation appears to be unconditional, "we seem impulsively driven to load up empty spaces, to plump some goddamn thing, any object, real, imagined, or otherwise, where now there might happily be nothing, a peaceful unsullied and unpeopled emptiness" (105). We ease our distress by setting aside the squirming facts in favor of a provisional government of meaning. Like the fireman who collects remnants of Klee's dentures, we invest the event with the requisite whys and wherefores to make it available to our reasoning and worthy of our reading time. (The story concludes with the author's apology for having taken up so much of our time for such meager rewards.)

The bulk of the narrative is devoted not to Klee but to Orval Nulin Evachefsky, who also ends by committing suicide by jumping off of a building. Compared to Klee, Orval is richly upholstered with personal history, and a discrete set of causes is developed to account for his killing himself. The causal arrangement is so satisfying that we would try to urge the Klee tale into similar slots, except that the confused bits of Klee that dot the pavement cannot even be assimilated into symbols, much less brought fully to life. His denture fragments "lie scattered over the pavement like . . . ah . . . like miniature milestones, let us say, marking the paths of his spilt life's blood. Well, we could say more, but the direction is dangerous" (110). Symbolism is habitual and tempting: couldn't we make something out of the Wilbur and Orval coincidence with the Wright brothers, who not only shared their names but were also flyers, albeit of a different sort? And what of the Klee/clay pun, or the connection with the abstract artist Paul Klee? As Ronald Sukenick recognizes in one of his self-conscious stories, "Connections proliferate, meanings drop away."[23] It would be nice if the scrap of paper that lies pinned by one of Klee's finger joints were part of a suicide note, or a clue to his personality, or legible, . . .

Truman Capote once said that the foundation of fiction is gossip, and Coover has seemed to carry that argument to a point far beyond that which Capote had intended. Out of the drift of words and the teasing patterns, there is nothing more substantial than gossip and rumor in "Klee Dead," a pointedly unpointed story. Scrounging the sidewalk for something identifiably human, each reader must piece together as much Klee as he can. It is an uncertain, grisly business.

With the writing of *Spanking the Maid*, scrutability is exchanged for comparatively modest goals: equilibrium, continuity, routine. Master and maid, locked in mutually dependent identities, are ostensibly striving to perfect their respective offices, which are determined for them by the ambiguous "manual." (It apparently defines not only her household duties and the appurtenances of servility, but also his sadomasochistic methods of urging her toward the ideal round of work.)

The anticipated sexual component of the spanking is complicated by the fact that both of them feel like victims of duties they do not relish. Indeed, the maid constantly has to administer to the welts and sores she contracts for her failures, and she grows anxious, not aroused, while awaiting punishment for the next damp towel or wrinkled sheet. Meanwhile, her master feels defeated despite diligent adherence to the rules of correction, and he dreams of release: "No, he would rather do just about anything else—crawl back into bed, read his manuals, even take a stroll in the garden—but he is committed to a higher end, his life a mission of sorts, a consecration, and so punish her he must, for to the extent that she fails, he fails."[24] We are reminded of the cycle of abuse that holds Hamm and Clov in Beckett's *Endgame*; in fact, Clov's "dream of order"—"all would be silent and still and each thing in its last place, under the last dust"[25]—anticipates the goal of Coover's maid.

Until perfection is earned, there is the abiding comfort of ritual to console chastiser and chastised alike; whereas Clov assumed that something, however mindless or wicked, was "taking its course," Coover's characters take greater responsibility for the plot that contains them. The master renews his dedication to "the purity of technique" (78) that guides his blows and sweeps out of consciousness the fantastic, riddling dreams he has each night. For her part, the maid silently surrenders herself to "the divine government of pain" (64) like a zealot to her God; she steadies herself with the faith that every shocking object she uncovers beneath the bedsheet—is she being tested?—and every brutal indignity at her master's hands is another step on the long road to spiritual improvement.

Efforts to pierce the surface of these repeated scenes end in frustration:

Sometimes, especially late in the day like this, watching the weals emerge from the blank page of her soul's ingress like secret writing, he finds himself searching for something, he doesn't know what exactly, a message of sorts, the revelation of a mystery in the spreading flush, in the pout and quiver of her cheeks, the repressed stutter of the little explosions of wind, the—whush—*SMACK!*—dew-bejeweled hieroglyphs of crosshatched stripes. But no, the futility of his labors, that's all there is to read there. (86–87)

So devotion must be honored for its own sake. And although each of the characters in *Spanking the Maid* is privately considering ending the rather vile farce, the very fact of continuity does have a look of profundity about it that neither wishes to dismiss so quickly. The relentlessness of this activity, however ugly, pornographic, or arbitrary, is their shared avenue to grace. And what about us readers, shouldering one another out of the way to get a better view of the proceedings, hoping against hope for a glimpse of purpose? Coover, that grinning magician and funhouse proprietor, shows his hand and enchants us anyway.

Patrick O'Donnell makes the point as part of a contrived dialogue about the inevitability and distortive nature of interpretive designs that readings may be inherently unsympathetic to the indeterminacy of their targets. Further, although we may long for a completed reading of events, consequences, or texts, analysis is at best a seemingly purgatorial series of rough drafts; and the tactics we bring to the task that prepare these events, consequences, or texts to achieve significant form merely embroider them with our own obsessions:

> *Hic:* Because it suggests that whenever we try to make an interpretive statement we are acting in bad faith by putting down what you describe as a mutable, dynamic movement.
> *Nunc:* That's quite true, and this discomfort or bad faith might be called the curse of writing, which always falsifies the process of interpretation. But, to rest in paradox, that falsification also creates another manifestation of the "literal," providing grounds for further interpretation.
> *Hic:* It makes one long for an impossible silence and simplicity.[26]

This yearning for a clean, well-lighted stasis, which precisely imitates Clov's dream of order, is delivered from the abyss of the free play of signification. A final interpretation, a comment like a valve that closes off discussion, or a silent peace "under the last dust" are, in the borderless realm of narrative, death wishes. Contemporary fiction, however, has another destiny in store for us: if not revelation, the rigors and riches of always moving toward.

Texts forge—create and dissemble. Codification libels experience. Scanning the blunt horizon for God's fingerprints, we establish epiphanies, then marvel at their ingenuity. But ingenuity connotes the corruptive powers of human intervention. Meanwhile, our hunger for the genuine saddles us with what Thomas Pynchon labels in *Gravity's Rainbow* "operational paranoia."[27]

As if in extreme reaction to this problem, the protagonist of Kenneth Gangemi's *OLT* seems indifferent to the inventories he compiles. Whereas plunges into the thickets of correlation aggravate Coover's characters, Olt retains an almost blissful inviolability. Depending on one's taste, he is either beyond agitation or hopelessly inert, sublime or exasperating. Perhaps his numbness can be understood as a deliberate defense against the disease of speculation that can only lead to anguish. More likely, it is the inevitable result of having been inundated for so long by details that resist incorporation into meaningful, or even digestible, patterns.

Thus, instead of composition, there is sheer apprehension of the discrete, atomized materials of contemporary life; no epiphany can coalesce. The novel opens with a parody of Stephen Dedalus's attempt to situate himself within, and at the center of, his universe; a breakdown of Man's species, genus, order, class, and phylum is offered without comment. It quickly gives way to the other nouns that clutter Olt's bureau: "a clipped advertisement that offered, for one dollar, a list of two hundred uses for sawdust, newspapers, and tin cans. There was a book about dinosaurs, a folder describing giant binoculars, a Japanese camera, a letter from a friend, a map of the city, a bear's tooth, and a list of forty-two differences between sunrises and sunsets."[28] It is impossible to determine which details, if any, are significant, illustrative, or portentous, for the "unplottedness" of the novel levels everything out. Experience does not assume any hierarchy of value, nor does it conform to any causal network as the novel progresses. Without interiority, metaphysical depth, or symbolic justification—all the components of "pseudo-mystery" to which we as readers have grown slavishly accustomed—what remains is a dehumanized verbal realm whose effect is to deny our habitual strategies of constructing emotional solidarity.[29]

The accumulation of undifferentiated material persists throughout the novel—a process of sedimentation, in which matters are occluded, not clarified. Olt has an unprecedented tolerance for being shown only the smooth surfaces of objects, facts, and other people. He reads incessantly, but he never falls into the conjectural quicksand that beleaguers more curious characters. No privileged moments take shape, for consciousness is utterly horizontal, its movements regular and unreflective:

> Robert Olt picked up the newspaper and began to read. Japan was building mineral-extracting ships that propelled themselves through the sea by ejecting the water they had processed. A gas explosion had blown off sixteen manhole

covers. The Pope had warned against "the virus of rationalism." A breed of chickens had been developed that laid nothing but double-yolked eggs.

The Marine Corps had hired a team of psychiatrists to find out why so many ex-marines went berserk. A physician had stated that one-third of the infant mortality rate was due to "irreducible birth and genetic accident." An avant-garde order of nuns had adopted a habit similar to the outfits of airline stewardesses. A filler said that Joe Hill died in front of a Utah firing squad. (43–44)

Olt's few sensations—vague abdominal pains, vague sexual urges—do not muster sufficient attention to be investigated, and they are subsumed within the general supersaturation of data. Ironically, the more information he filters, the greater our sense of his impoverishment. *OLT* concludes with a list of missed opportunities, and the effect is at once comical and elegiac:

> Olt knew he would never see a meteor striking an iceberg, a bat falling into snow, or a clown on a nun. He knew he would never go to a party and talk to thunderstorm experts, roller-coaster experts, vampire experts, sailplane experts, dinosaur experts, or volcano experts. He knew he would never design bear grottos, furnish a time capsule, live in an orange grove, wade in a vat of mercury, work in the Dead Letter Office, find narwhale tusks on a beach, see a tampax string at the ballet, smell a burning spice warehouse, overhear two call girls talking shop, or attend a meeting of the Junior League.
>
> Olt knew he would never find a purse containing birth-control pills, sketching pencils, and *Les Fleurs du Mal*; see a slow-motion film of bullets striking a condemned man's chest and face; look through an illustrated 1898 brothel-supplier's catalogue; ride on top of a narrow-gauge banana train winding slowly through the jungle; make a training film for prostitutes; see a corpse crushed in a giant hydraulic press; hear Mozart's *Symphony #42* or read *Orwell in Mexico*; see impoverished citizens getting free passes to government brothels; sit on an Alaskan riverbank and eat salmon with eagles and bears; see the woman with the biggest bush in the world; read the *Mars Daily News* while sitting on the trimmed lawn of the University of Venus; see hundreds of naked pregnant women floating on their backs in Great Salt Lake. (49–50)

What "meganovels" like *The Recognitions, Gravity's Rainbow,* or *LETTERS* take several hundred pages to realize, *OLT* confirms in fifty: the futility of trying "to reproduce the world in an isolated heterocosm."[30] Furthermore, as the "nevers" multiply, what Olt does not experience, and what he does, become indistinguishable in our minds, for the flat manner of presentation remains constant. In other words, the surfaces of remembered, read about, and imagined events—or rather, the facts and clauses that substitute for events—are the same: everything is detached, and everything is equally unredemptive.

Olt's world is coolly eclectic. Gangemi wages a war on "aboutness." The "appointment" upon which the novel presumably centers is missed; we are seduced into anticipating a possible suicide, but that, too, is aborted. Horrors, wonders, aberrations, and dreams are ground together into a dispassionate democracy of trivia—a roll call of fragments.

Olt parodies Henry James's ideal artist on whom nothing is lost, for Olt merely hoards without absorbing or analyzing. The novel is all carpet and no figure, or, to use another of James's phrases, *OLT* does not press beyond "the gross rattle of the foreground."[31] Despite his talent for accumulation, Olt is incapable of possession, as though the quotation from Rilke he carries—"And one has nothing and nobody / and one travels about the world / with a trunk and a case of books" (52)—were a creed of alienation.

What is the syntax of experience? *OLT* speaks the debris of contemporary culture and adds itself to it. As to the pleasures of this text, we may turn for explanation to William Gass, for whom the march of catalogues is celebrational:

> Lists, then, are for those who savor, who revel and wallow, who embrace, not only the whole of things, but all of its accounts, histories, descriptions, justifications. They are for those who like, in every circumstance, to Thomas Wolfe things down, to whoop it, Whitmanly, up. . . . Even the jeremiad is a list, and full of joy, for damnations are delightful. Lists are finally for those who love language, the vowel-swollen cheek, the lilting, dancing tongue, because lists are fields full of words, and roving bands of "and."[32]

The tradition in realistic fiction is to smuggle symbols smoothly by us and to render descriptive passages in such a way that they do not interfere with the "natural flow" of the narrative.[33] But in novels like *OLT*, whose meaning is limited to the surface tension of its lists, these passages strip themselves of such disguise and openly sun themselves for pages at a time. In this way, "as the novelist's art became artful, the novel's previous attention to detail, its love of ethical, psychological, and sociological analysis, its simpering sentimentalities and lubricious teasing, its dreary derring-do and wild-eyed running up and down on roads, is replaced, without altering anything but the aim of our attention, by *words*."[34]

Gangemi's novel rummages through the world but refrains from evaluating its contents; Olt is tirelessly inspecting but seldom introspective.

Words do not further examination of their references. Rather, words constitute their own depthless collage. Like gleaming shells on the beach, they stand forth as individualized objects; as William Carlos Williams suggests when he speaks of the transforming powers of poetry, words are "inimitable particles of dissimilarity to all other things."[35] Only when the word is extracted from typical contexts and our rage for association is quelled does "its own reality establish its own freedom from the necessity of a word, thus freeing it and dynamizing it at the same time."[36]

Because Olt does not strive, or manage, to perceive symmetries among the items he collects, he himself remains a blur, for only by virtue of a subjective involvement with his world would he be prominently featured within it.[37] Since he is merely a passive receptor instead of an expressive composer, Olt is victimized, as it were, by having so thoroughly vanquished the romance of signification through which the ego typically asserts its indispensability.

The stark, solid language of the novel has its own gravitational pull, and nothing—no instructive relationships, and surely no transcendent revelation—escapes the textual orbit. Because everything is words, and all words are manufactured from the same "script," everything is equally synthetic. Thus, instead of progressive understanding, *OLT* presents a more circumscribed brand of intrigue: that of the notoriety of individual molecules within a monotonous verbal landscape. Olt never emerges from the general drift.

The widespread default of postmodern fiction on the convention of "the 'finalist determination' of narrative"[38] reveals the strategies through which we accustom ourselves to texts by making us complicit in the making of meaning even as the means for achieving closure are discredited. The more rigorously Gilbert Sorrentino's *Odd Number* extorts itself for reliable meaning, the more contradictory and insupportable its "confessions" become. Once again, we are witness to the demolition of the empirical method that would flush epiphany out of hiding. Because he insists on engaging narrative non-symbolically, or anti-symbolically, Sorrentino adheres to a dream of a "signalless American novel" that resists metaphorical, and even referential, pretensions.[39]

Odd Number is a three-part inquisition of its own fragile premises, and it cracks under the strain:

> I haven't told you anything that's a n y t h i n g this these all these papers this testimony and data and reports eyewitness reports anonymous reports these transcripts and depositions and God! diaries this crap this shit you ask and I

answer and always almost always before I can finish you ask some more and some more and some more and I find or try to find something that will do that will answer if you think that what all this is all this is is just some from some fucking novel why don't you read the novel and get all the answers right there?[40]

Part One of the novel asks thirty-three questions of a furtive, panting respondent who is helplessly befuddled despite (or because of) his having apparently gathered huge quantities of material evidence—diaries, memoranda, photographs, rumors, and testimonies—in preparation for this debriefing. After his sputtering comes the swarm of Part Two, which employs the very same questions in reverse order but now poses them to a glib, gossipy speaker; not only do his answers fail to correspond to those exacted from his tentative predecessor, but because he is more proficient in his evasions (especially regarding the obscure circumstances surrounding the death of one Sheila Henry), his banter actually increases our suspicions instead of allaying them. Both respondents disclaim responsibility for their respective "readings" of the situation: the first complains that he cannot vouch for the accuracy of the written records, and after all, he was not actually there at the events in question, nor did he know the principal characters involved; the second, who had the advantages lacked by the first, suggests that we might do better to enlist the aid of someone with "real" information—hard documentary evidence—and anyway, none of this is really his business. Thus, as the structure of the novel doubles back upon itself, so too does its content obliterate gains painstakingly achieved earlier.

Part Three features a comparatively objective, or objective-sounding, respondent. The interrogator (our proxy-critic within the novel) still relies on the catechism method, but he has switched to a different set of questions, perhaps because of the confusions resulting from the first set. Whatever initial relief this last respondent's tone offers soon dissipates, however, as we realize that it derives from fictions, Sorrentino having cannibalized his earlier works for personalities and premises in *Odd Number*. Instead of a consolidation of perspectives around a core truth (say, in the manner of Faulkner's *The Sound and the Fury*), *Odd Number* consists of a series of decentered, competing fabrications. Although the degree of self-avowedness among them may vary, we never approach conviction.[41] And because it implies a privileged witness, epiphany is frustrated by the anti-hierarchical textual premise.

This letdown is concomitant with the reassessment of the language's capacity for containing and delivering experience. Like Coover, Sorrentino foregrounds his misgivings over the referentiality of words. In a review of the writings of Maurice Blanchot, Sorrentino highlights Blanchot's declaration regarding the treachery of the medium they share: "Language perceives that its meaning derives not from what exists, but from its retreat from existence."[42] In a "readerly" text, to borrow Roland Barthes's terms, the configuration of events and motives (the characters' as well as the author's) emerges like bones through the subtle skin of the story and compensates our reading with an authentic—or at least, consensual—version. In *Odd Number,* on the contrary, the facts never escape the distorting context of how we know what we know about the facts. No synthetic conception of how or whether the deceptions referred to in the novels can arise out of the narratives that constitute them. In this sense, any individual reading of *Odd Number* merely adds another deposition to the proceedings, while the colon that "concludes" the novel implies that future interpretations are anticipated and inevitable.

By the time the third respondent contends that no murder has occurred at all, we have ceased to depend upon more neutral witnesses or more judicious questions to lead us out of ignorance. Instead, the meandering discourse itself is the case at hand, for language is simultaneously the foundation for and the destination of the investigation. As Michel Foucault admonishes us:

> The existence of systems of rarefaction does not imply that, over and beyond them lie great vistas of limitless discourse, continuous and silent, repressed and driven back by them, making it our task to abolish them and at last to restore it to speech. When talking in terms of speaking or thinking, we must not imagine some unsaid thing, or an unthought floating about the world, interlacing with all its forms and events. Discourse must be treated as a discontinuous activity, its different manifestations sometimes coming together, but just as easily unaware of, or excluding, each other.[43]

William Carlos Williams, a prodigious influence on Sorrentino, explains the sort of negative capability that the unruly tide of self-referential language requires: "The wish would be to see not floating visions of unknown purport but the imaginative qualities of actual things being perceived accompany their gross vision in a slow dance, interpreting as they go. But inasmuch as this will not always be the case one must dance nevertheless as he can."[44] Once he has renegotiated his responsibility to external reality, the postmodern writer can likewise elude the causative presumptions that in realistic fiction exist prior to the individual instance of language. Repudiating such basic prerequisites for detection as stable character and consistent data plunges us into Freud's realm of the "uncanny," as defined in the Epigraph to *Odd Number* according to the trackless vicissitudes of substitution, division, and repetition.

Also under indictment in the novel are the mimetic aspirations of the various media subscribed to by their respondents: the shuffled transcripts, reports, and dossiers. Their dysfunctions, compounded by the inability to refine characters out of the movie, the roman à clef, the whispered secrets, and the previous books by Sorrentino that include them as well, transform the would-be empiricist into Heisenberg's uncertain scientist, or a fetishist: "I can't imagine who'd want to know this, some sort of sick mind prodding and poking into people's lives this one, 'The Party' you can look through it, every scrap and what you'll find out is what I found" (5–6). The more aggressive the analysis, the more the same ground is plowed under, and the less likely an understanding can be based upon it:

> what can I say? you get ten or twenty or fifty people who know each other and you're bound to get coincidences and all sorts of odd what's the word I'm looking for? alliances no not alliances though alliances is all right but I can't seem to say call them configurations it seems to me that with your questions and doubts and going back over the same ground you're complicating things more than it is a maze I agree but I'm trying to give you what I have (25)

Eventually, *Odd Number* chokes on its own repetitions. The novel does not build to a climax but instead attenuates to a colon like a washed-out bridge (159). Maybe the respondents *are* cooperating; it is the business of relating bit to slippery bit—the tactics of approximation—that is "bad as life." By the time the dispassionate, reproving third respondent declares that the first had really been the third and the second the fifth and derides all systematizing as sheer finesse, we feel out of our depth altogether: "If the catalogue, or any catalogue or list, is understood to be a system, its entropy is the measure of the unavailability of its energy for conversion into useful work" (156). We are at the mercy of an endless host of impeachable sources. *Odd Number* trades on the old shell game of Truth; Sorrentino shuffles the cups before our eyes but knows full well that there is no pea beneath any of them. Or better still, there are as many peas as players to probe for them.

Wallace Stevens's "Sunday Morning" complains of a sky deserted by divinity. As they are conventionally manifested in literature, our teleological urges disdain the implications of "this dividing and indifferent blue"[45] and promote causal rigor and interpretive design. We have learned to depend upon the author to endow the art with continuity and conse- quence, to ensure "the gluey whine of connectedness"[46] so that human aspiration fuels aesthetic projects. But everywhere postmodern fiction meticulously hedges its bets against a single, sanctified reading of experi- ence that would reward epiphanic aspirations.

The High Modernist reaction to indeterminacy, as ascribed to Joyce by Eliot, was to prepare "a way of controlling, of ordering, of giving a shape and a significance to the immense panorama of futility and anarchy which is contemporary history."[47] From that imperial height, the artist perceived portentous depth. The contemporary reaction, on the other hand, has been to acknowledge the inevitable corruption of the observer by the ambiguity of phenomenal reality. In the words of Alfred North White- head, "All explanations must end in an ultimate arbitrariness."[48] Dogma- tism, however inspired, is either arrogant or naive. As Saul Bellow's Sammler acidly considers, "You had to be a crank to insist on being right. . . . The soul sat unhappily on superstructures of explanation, poor bird, not knowing which way to fly."[49]

Metaphysical speculation runs aground against physical, philosophical, and linguistic limitations. For example, contemporary scientific models have largely rendered the pretense of secure, objective measurement ob- solete: "Because everything, in the field view, is connected to everything else by means of the mediating field, the autonomy assigned to individual events by language is illusory. When the field is seen to be inseparable from language, the situation becomes even more complex, for then every statement potentially refers to every other statement, including itself."[50] Applying the effects of this impasse to the entrapment of language within its own structural habits and priorities, according to which the questions we put to existence never escape the linguistic and cultural realities that shape and implicate all discourse, "external reality" cannot be approached through literary means (and may well be a contradiction in terms). If Einstein and Heisenberg contend that intervention alters the object of analysis, Foucault and Barthes (who defines a literary work as "a question put to language") surmise that no verifiable intervention even takes place, in that language only presents itself.[51]

Insights that behave according to the dictates of language are held in tow as soon as they are generated; the literary work is inescapably hermetic and local. By extension, that which surpasses understanding lies beyond the grasp of a verbal system. As Susan Sontag writes, "Even the simplest sensation is, in its totality, indescribable. . . . Stylistic devices are also techniques of avoidance."[52] We are unsettled by the "indecorous" tendency of postmodern fiction to foreground its failure to get itself precisely, adequately said. Meanwhile, the ineffable looms like some monolithic possibility around which words slowly curl. The shape of truth is only suggested by fiction as it contends with its absence.

Perhaps these disruptions of how we think about the relationship between literature and the world have helped to immunize contemporary readers against epiphanic expectations. But the question remains whether a brand of fiction that does not transcend the status quo serves to endorse it. Moreover, if "meaning is not the exclusive property of narrative resolutions,"[53] are there more or less proper or effective means of maneuvering in the midst of meanings that arise otherwise? A "justification" of anti-epiphanic fiction demands that we view art not as a formal disclosure of meaning but as an exploration of the conditions under which meaning is accomplished. In other words, with the illusion of a totalized reading debunked and the wedding of referent and reference annulled, "the highest reality lies in a consciousness which reveals its very limitations. The game is 'won' when such consciousness is achieved."[54] Anti-epiphanic fiction assembles more than it develops, performs more than it deciphers. Revelatory impulses are either absent or confessed to be literary conventions. The search for synthesis declines into an acceptance of syntheticism.

What dark grammar guides our going? Perhaps we must first ask how fiction that refuses to acknowledge epiphanic functions reciprocates our attention. Impatient to translate "the coarse flow" of human currents into a stable icon, readers who insist that their stories redeem life from ambiguity are like Tchitcherine in *Gravity's Rainbow*, who tries to superimpose the laws of a "shaped, cleaned, rectified" alphabet onto experience.[55] Such readers will find the staunchly anti-climactic nature of the literature under discussion intolerable. In place of essentialist comforts, we are offered a plea for integrity—fiction can dispense with the illusion of suspended disbelief—and a challenge to the reader to participate in the creation of textual realities. Borrowing Ronald Sukenick's terminology, we are asked to exchange "thought" for "thinking," which prefers the tentative, ongoing, improvisational process of invention to the definition of the work of art as an achieved end.[56]

Instead of the premeditated form, there is the mediating performance, and one of the consequences is a "democratized" negotiation of meaning, which may be the postmodern author's compensation for lost authority. Of course, not every contemporary writer handles this dispossession so blithely as Sukenick. Alan Wilde suspects that "the mangled shadow of significant form falls raggedly across the page" in even the most stylistically playful of recent fictions, and that "the ordering coercions of the artist's subjectivity" continue to operate.[57] But the time for innocently confusing the rage for order with its reliable discovery has apparently passed. In the examples we have witnessed, postmodern speculation is largely a matter of textual provocation, while our little lives are rounded with a sleep.

> "No wonder kids grow up crazy. A cat's cradle is nothing but a bunch of X's between someone's hands, and little kids look and look and look at all those X's . . ."
> "And?"
> *"No damn cat, and no damn cradle."*[58]

Chapter 3

Deregulating Histories

> Only for the egoist and the dogmatist (and maybe they're
> one and the same, although I'm thinking of two different
> friends of mine) is there one "history" only. The rest of us
> live with the suspicion that there are as many histories as
> there are people and maybe a few more—out here in the
> flood, after all . . . what arrangements can we *not* imagine?
>
> —from *What Ever Happened to Gloomy Gus
> of the Chicago Bears?*, by Robert Coover

> I *would* like to try to tell such a story, if he means the kind
> that begins: "There was a woman . . ." followed by plot, the
> absolute line between two points which I've always despised.
> Not for literary reasons, but because it takes all hope away.
> Everyone, real or invented, deserves the open destiny of life.
>
> —from "A Conversation with My Father," by Grace Paley

> The sum of history became in his head no more than the
> stuff of metaphors.
>
> —from *The Sot-Weed Factor*, by John Barth

> Give historical intention a natural justification, make con-
> tingency appear eternal. . . . Think of page as timber line.
> Between reality and men, between description and explana-
> tion, between object and knowledge.
>
> —from *Ketjak*, by Ron Silliman

Credibility is an ever-expanding field. In 1960 Philip Roth wrote his
sardonic complaint that the writer of fiction has to compete with an
American reality whose outrages far exceed anything writers could fab-
ricate, as though the daily news had annexed territory that once had been
reserved for the novelist.[1] What is now fashionably referred to as today's
"information society" intensifies Roth's predicament, for it is virtually
overloaded with "such diverse and disparate views of reality that no single
interpretive frame can contain them all and still present a coherent vision
of experience."[2] In our common state of perplexity, we are apt to recall I.
B. Singer's Gimpel the Fool, who, having grown so weary of encounters

with lies masquerading as truths, concludes that "the world is entirely an imaginary world" and envisions a heaven scrubbed clean of illusion: "When my time comes I will go joyfully. Whatever may be there, it will be real, without complication, without ridicule, without deception. God be praised: there even Gimpel cannot be deceived."[3]

When we locate a given work of fiction on the spectrum whose conventional poles are Realism and Anti-Realism, our characterization of that work is decided by its attitude toward, and means of appropriation of, extratextual reality. However, this sort of evaluation presumes a definition of reality that is, if not monolithic and static, at least accessible and distinguishable from the fiction at hand. And, as we have seen, any definition of reality that ignores its fictional underpinnings is either naive or despotic.

One profound feature of contemporary American fiction is its equal skepticism toward statements derived from both fictional and historical contexts: not only is fiction confessed as artifice, but the history out of which it emerges and from which it presumably departs is exposed as relying upon fictional methods and strategies, thereby revealing history to be one more realm of discourse stripped of privilege. In the previous chapter, we saw how the world fluoresces at the touch of language, as though a clause were actually a conjuring and a metaphor a laying on of hands. As a supreme network of ordering principles, one which has the additional distinction of public acceptance and extensive documentation, history is more deceptive in its employment of fiction's charms and fabrications but by no means free of them.

Accordingly, the historian and the novelist face the same problem of shaping recalcitrant material into expressive form, and their comparable enterprises provoke a series of obstacles that are foregrounded in recent fiction. For example, since all systems of organizing and selecting evidence are falsifications, any stabilizing perspective, any representation "of life halted and poised for analysis,"[4] must be indicted for its distortions; in place of T. S. Eliot's "complete consort dancing together,"[5] we are confronted with limited, local aptitudes for making sense of things. Next arises the problem of language itself, for language promotes its own structural "mandates" that interfere with, or at least obscure, the transmission of meaning. And if we supplant the structures of the world with configurations of the mind, on what basis are the genuine and the spurious to be differentiated?

These very issues, which are commonplaces of literary criticism, have also come to bear upon the study of history, as a number of contemporary historians have converged upon the literary basis of historical "narrative."[6] The most celebrated among them is probably Hayden White, who in his *Metahistory* and *Tropics of Discourse* delineates the narrative priorities through which the historian stipulates the order of experience. White maintains that our passion for intelligibility prescribes styles of historical writing that mandate such explanatory techniques as emplotment, formal argument, and ideological implication that "prefigure" the experiential field. As this terminology indicates, these procedures, through which the domain under investigation is not merely described but constituted, is poetic in nature:

> In short, the historian's problem is to construct a linguistic protocol, complete with lexical, grammatical, syntactical, and semantic dimensions, by which to characterize the field and its elements *in his own terms* . . . and thus to prepare them for the explanation and representation he will subsequently offer of them in his narrative.[7]

Thus, language determines the conditions under which historical events *mean*—indeed, by which events are identified *as* events. Coherence displaces correspondence as an evaluative measure of a given historical account, so that an error is not only a lapse in verifiability but a failure to live up to the aesthetic requirements of the constructive, selective, and integrative impulses that instigated that account. Moreover, just as the realistic novel has been debunked for its naive presumptions regarding the reliable transmission of reality through the faithful and transparent medium of language, and has been contested by the self-conscious postrealist novel with its confessions of artifice, so too has historical writing undergone a reappraisal that reveals how its descriptions are actually constructions. What is sought, in effect, is not a totalized Truth per se but a psychologically adequate "encoding" of reality.[8] "What the historian must bring to his consideration of the record are general notions of the *kinds of stories* that might be found there," says White, "just as he must bring to consideration of the problem of narrative representation some notion of the 'pre-generic plot-structure' by which the story *he* tells is endowed with formal coherency."[9] Louis O. Mink concurs, declaring that history and fiction offer the same lessons in "how to tell and to understand *complex* stories, and how it is that stories answer questions."[10] Both White and Mink appear to take their cue from R. G. Collingwood, who advocates the importance of an historical imagination that does not passively accept a supply of details from the past but, like the novelist, actively demands whatever would contribute to the sense he intends to make of it.[11] History joins fiction in being more overtly purposive than previous assumptions of its impartial documentation allow. In either case, a narrative is colored by the desires of its author to plug holes with wholes—a claim Hayden White substantiates when he explains that the historian must write fiction in order to imbue "his account of the past with the odor of meaning or significance."[12] That the historian addresses pre-existent material—characters, settings, and actions with real-world status that precedes his fictional operations—while the novelist invents does not alter the compatibility of their methods of "exclusion, stress, and subordination" through which particular kinds of stories are reified out of the turbulence of potentialities:

> Here the historians must utilize precisely the same tropological strategies, the same modalities of representing relationships in words, that the poet or novelist uses. In the unprocessed historical record and in the chronicle of events which the historian extracts from the record, the facts exist only as a congeries of contiguously related fragments. . . . These fragments are put together in the same ways that novelists use to put together fragments of their imaginations to display an ordered world, a cosmos, where only disorder or chaos might appear.[13]

The elusiveness of Truth empowers the historian to inscribe it according to his needs even as it underscores the ultimate provisionality and incompleteness of his creation. Whereas history is thereby "democratized," in that authority over its making is available to an infinite number of interpretations (and interpreters), it is also demoted by virtue of the revelation of its insufficiency in face of the fullness of experience.[14] A dogmatic reading of experience would not only transgress against "the suggestion of doubt as to its own authority" that all genuine discourse "systematically displays on its surface,"[15] it could lead to the degeneration of fiction into a totalitarian myth demanding "absolute assent"—a condition that is at once aesthetically and politically intolerable.[16] (One sublime example of this imperialistic domination of language, imagery, and meaning is embodied as the military bureaucracy whose coercive mentality is status quo in Joseph Heller's *Catch-22*.)

The often-vexing alternative is what Cushing Strout terms a "contemporary agnosticism" regarding all products of the imagination, all of which are subject to the strictures of literary criticism moreso than to those of scientific inquiry.[17] It has been argued that in the wake of the notorious expulsion of history that characterized Modernist fiction,[18] contemporary fiction ventures to reintroduce history by recognizing its availability to fictional devices. But again, this is not to be confused with a reconciliation between textual ambiguities and an authentic, extra-textual bedrock; on the contrary, it represents a mutual, unranked contextualization of occasions of discourse. As Roland Barthes is quick to assert, the linguistic character of history—historical reality is a human construction, a man-made significance—must be acknowledged if we are to avoid idolizing culturally sanctioned accounts of "what really happened" and so relinquish our freedom to make meaning.[19]

This situation enables the historian-heroes of several recent American novels to participate in the "voicing" of reality by imaginatively projecting themselves onto it in a campaign for personal relevance, even as it automatically appears to trivialize their efforts and to underscore the insufficiency of *any* interpretation to assimilate and harmonize the hostile swarm of data and detail.

Hayden White insists, "What is at issue here is not, What are the facts? but rather, How are the facts to be described in order to sanction one mode of explaining them rather than another?"[20] E. L. Doctorow complements this position when he claims that "there is no history except as it is composed" and that "history shares with fiction a mode of mediating the world for the purpose of introducing meaning, and it is the cultural authority from which they both derive that illuminates those facts so that they can be perceived."[21] Throughout his novels we discover individuals who oppose the determinations of institutional powers that have arrogated to themselves the techniques of the novelist, and this opposition takes the form of attempts to recreate more hospitable, just and forgiving versions of history. Doctorow finds such activities to be necessarily subversive, for they challenge the imperious rule of the "consensus of sensibility" and contest "a regime language that derives its strength from what we are supposed to be" by positing "a language of freedom whose power consists in what we threaten to become."[22]

The Book of Daniel is especially devoted to the linguistic grounds of political struggle, and a great deal has been written regarding the angle of departure in that novel from the historical facts of the Rosenberg case. From a broader perspective, *The Book of Daniel* is a systematic assault on the very concept of verifiability, a condition that, while it stymies the empiricist, liberates the artist by affording him (Daniel Isaacson) the opportunity to revise the "consensus of sensibility" and, in the form of his narrative inquiry, to reopen the case—ultimately, to manufacture a new verdict for his parents. Richard Poirier's description of "performance" writing neatly approximates this verbal "exercise of power," which he concedes to be narcissistic in its impetuosity and urgency but not solipsistic because it is "so eager for publicity, love, and historical dimension. Out of an accumulation of secretive acts emerges at last a form that presumes to compete with reality for control of the minds exposed to it."[23] The historian Carl L. Becker similarly anticipates Daniel's motives when he describes the "existential" challenge to each new generation of historians as having to "play on the dead whatever tricks it finds necessary for its own peace of mind."[24]

But Daniel does not succumb to the doctrinaire prerogative assumed by the "regime." His narrative inquiry interrogates its own machinations as relentlessly as it does those of the official record: "Life is never this well-plotted"[25] is a qualification that equally applies to the version of the guilt of Paul and Rochelle Isaacson perpetrated by the ruling class and to the conspiracy unearthed by Daniel himself.

Each of Doctorow's novels destabilizes the composition it presents in this very manner, undermining the artist's "imitation with words of the tangible real world of act and event and thunder" that appear capable of reformulating that world according to the desires of its witness.[26] The narrator's admission of the unsteadiness of his account represents an acceptance of moral obligation even at the expense of his story. "Political language *is* political reality," maintains political scientist Murray Edelman; "there is no other so far as the meaning of events to actor and spectators is concerned."[27] So a deceptive manipulation of our experience of that language is surely as available to Daniel as it is to White House spokespersons or Orwellian Newspeakers. Were Daniel to insist upon his own thesis (we remember that he is ostensibly at work on his doctoral dissertation), Daniel might well be held to blame for a kind of small-scale despotism; he would be imitating governmental restrictiveness of the scope of expression and would therefore be violating the ethical principles that in large measure are responsible for his attempting his revisionist "book" in the first place. In the words of Michel Foucault, "Humanity installs each of its violences in a system of linguistic rules and thus proceeds from domination to domination,"[28] and these manipulations are theoretically available to anyone wishing to "author" them. Because this would be artistically and politically unconscionable, Daniel speculates but does not dictate. *The Book of Daniel* retains a commitment to open-endedness and unresolved possibility—Daniel is painfully aware of how bureaucratic resolutions can be personal impasses—and champions this condition for its conduciveness to narrative incursion. As Geoffrey Galt Harpham points out, "The factor of plausibility introduces a fictional element into the description that confirms the novelistic enterprise." Since no one version of the Isaacson case can be more than plausible, the images that emerge from Daniel's analysis "shimmer" with latency; however, once those images become "tightly bound," their potential hardened and finalized, they "tend toward totalitarianism."[29]

Doctorow has remained faithful in each of his novels to what we might call the integrity of irresolution. Blue, the self-appointed town chronicler in *Welcome to Hard Times,* is perhaps Doctorow's supreme example of the paralyzing self-consciousness that this creed may foster. He continually complains that his attempt to "put down what happened" is as much a "poor pinched-out claim" as the other optimistic myths—the hope of the frontier, man's superior capacity for civilization over destructive violence, the saving grace of posterity—that disintegrate in the course of the novel. Disclaimers and recriminations nibble at the edges of the sense he tries to make of the disaster:

> The form remembrance puts on things is making its own time and guiding my pen in ways I don't trust.

> I'm losing my blood to this rag, but more, I have the cold feeling everything I've written down doesn't tell how it was, no matter how careful I've been to get it all down it still escapes me: like what happened is far below my understanding beyond my sight. In my limits, taking a day for a day, a night for a night, have I showed the sand shifting under our feet, the terrible arrangement of our lives?

> And now I've put down what happened, everything that happened from one end to the other. And it scares me more than death scares me that it may show the truth. But how can it if I've written as if I knew as I lived them which minutes were important and which not; and spoken as if I knew the exact words everyone spoke? Does the truth come out in such scrawls, so bound by my limits?[30]

"Nothing fixes in this damned country": not societies, not sentences. In an environment where gunfire is real and talk evaporates in the wind's roar, Blue scorns himself "for a fool for all the bookkeeping I've done; as if notations in a ledger can fix life, as if some marks in a book can control things."[31] The notion of fixing life—arresting it or repairing it—is but a seduction of language, and Blue believes he is not artist enough to carry it off anyway.

Doctorow himself echoes Philip Roth's concession in "Writing American Fiction" when he says that American society is "such an immense place and almost—in all its great, whirling self-destruction—impossible to make a metaphor of."[32] He restates this attitude in his short story "The Foreign Legation" in the mind of his embittered protagonist: "It interested him that something so untrue to life could be life."[33] In *The Book of Daniel*, then, Daniel's compulsion to manufacture a history that might exonerate his family cannot be answered with finality for two reasons: a paradigmatic reading of the events comprised by his parents' case would be "untrue to life," which is identified by multifariousness and ambiguity; and the advocacy of a domineering thesis of Daniel's own, however more appealing than the thesis promoted by the State, would necessitate Daniel's cooptation by the "regime" style against which he has pitted himself—Daniel would still be a victim of political diction. (At times Daniel does exhibit tyrannical behavior in his sadistic sexual advances toward his wife, and of course, it is here that someone whose motive is to elicit sympathy is least sympathetic.) So in order to be true to the ambiguity of the realities it confronts, *The Book of Daniel* must be more or less comprehensible but never masquerade as comprehensive; the integrity of the narrative is not measured by its authoritativeness but by its anti-illusionist rigor and its willingness to testify without flinching, as is most tellingly displayed when Daniel undertakes the task of depicting the electrocutions of Paul and Rochelle. He "executes" them, both in the sense of recapitulating their deaths and in the sense of rendering them, or embracing them, in the full, contemplative circle of the book.

"The failure to make connections is complicity" (227) is Daniel's motto and incentive, but even the analysis that results requires deconstruction; otherwise, the analyst is complicit in the making of seamless fictions for which he indicts the purveyors of conventional wisdom. "For it is perhaps the hallmark of the historian's craft (or of the understanding of history as a craft)," writes Dominick LaCapra, "to construct encyclopedically exhaustive and 'definitive' accounts upon relatively unexamined assumptions about the use of language" to the neglect of "the goal-oriented, unifying center of vision or . . . the decentered subject as the mobile prism of diffraction. . . ."[34] Like Dreiser seeking a "proper alignment" for his chair or Peary scrabbling about the ice cap trying to "find the exact spot to say this spot, here, is the North Pole" in *Ragtime*,[35] Daniel oscillates between first- and third-person point of view and shifts from dissertation to lyric to documentary to political tract to diary to confession, changing his lenses and adapting his focus like a "little criminal of perception" (34).

Writing is sedition. One must rebel against the Establishment's symbolic manipulation that casts him in the role of victim or cipher or outlaw. This is the harsh light Artie Sternlicht casts upon the Isaacsons: "Instead of standing up and saying fuck you, do what you want, I can't get an honest trial anyway with you fuckers—they made motions, they pleaded innocent, they spoke only when spoken to, they played the game. All right? The whole frame of reference brought them down because they acted like defendants at a trial" (151). It is almost awe-inspiring how the system works to dispel contradiction. "One cannot help being thrilled by the virtually automatic engagement of every self-protective capacity of our civilization,"[36] and history becomes in Thomas Pynchon's phrase, "at best, a conspiracy, not always among gentlemen, to defraud."[37] The hegemonizing strategies of the ruling class insist that the Isaacsons be found guilty because they are *founded* as guilty, defined as sacrificial like the rest of America's radical left.[38]

Nevertheless, Daniel learns that success is not a matter of supplanting one history with another but rather the result of situating himself within history in order to expose its maneuvers. In their disparate methods, Artie Sternlicht (in his rhetorical subterfuge), Linda Mindish (in her deliberate refusal to entertain potentially damaging interpretations of her father's involvement in the conspiracy), Walt Disney (in his "sentimental compression" of American history), and even, symbolically, the man who works in the subway change booth who Daniel suspects is so insulated that he won't even feel it when a bomb drops, all exemplify artists in bad faith, for they are wilfully reductive in the service of self-protective, self-justifying myths.[39] On the other hand, were Daniel merely to carve out an autonomous enclave for himself—an autotelic empire on the order of a staunchly hermetic, anti-referential novel—his activity would cease to be politically responsible and would in fact corroborate his suspicion that he had been robbed of the ability to be dangerous (as evidenced by the ineffectiveness of his burning his draft card during a Viet Nam protest rally, given that the son of the Isaacsons would never face conscription anyway); such a weak-willed escape from domination might well become an end in itself, politically ineffective and insubstantial to pit against the Establishment as either a threat or a model of transformation. Clearly it is not enough for Daniel to mitigate his family legacy of "causing public commotion" (13) in the hope of securing anonymity beyond the infiltrations of journalists, psychologists, and the FBI; to stop there would be to impersonate the Inertia Kid at the Children's Shelter or the deathly fate of the Starfish, the lost sign of the zodiac that, like Daniel's suicidal sister, is doomed to implode. His mission is to save the Isaacsons from the absolute history with which the state has saddled them.

Cushing Strout writes in *The Veracious Imagination*, "It is appropriate for the novelist to focus not on the public consequences of the agent's deeds, but rather upon their personal meaning for his own salvation."[40] Indeed, Daniel struggles to interpolate personal meaning as public consequence by producing a "novel as private I" (269). Accordingly, he must continually cite and contest the "canonized" findings; however, he must never insist on any one interpretation, only on the condition of interpretability as a perpetual option. *The Book of Daniel* grants access to other readings—documents, interviews, and the like—so as to disrupt their established stature. Doctorow suggests that the susceptibility of these findings to interrogation is characteristic of "the most important trials in our history":

> those which reverberate in our lives and have most meaning for our future, are those in which the judgment is called into question: Scopes, Sacco and Vanzetti, the Rosenbergs. Facts are buried, exhumed, deposed, contradicted, recanted. There is a decision by the jury and, when the historical and prejudicial context of the decision is examined, a subsequent judgment by history. And the trial shimmers forth with just that perplexing ambiguity characteristic of a true novel.[41]

Daniel's effort to redeem the family name centers upon the hypothesis that a second couple was actually responsible for the crimes of espionage, whereby Paul Isaacson and Selig Mindish, his treasonous friend who sold him out, are primarily guilty of covering up for the escaped criminals:

> But this isn't the couple in the poster. That couple got away. Well funded, and supplied with false passports, they went either to New Zealand or Australia. Or Heaven. In any event, my mother and father, standing in for them, went to their deaths for crimes they did not commit. (42)

To be sure, this argument is in keeping with evidence uncovered by other historians, which is to admit that the Rosenberg case is no more consistently edifying than the Isaacson case that imaginatively succeeds it.[42] Daniel's hypothesis does return the infamous Isaacsons to the familiar orbit of the mundane radio repairman and his wife, whom Daniel has so much trouble recognizing in their massive, grotesque, media-created identities. Nevertheless, Daniel does not propose his hypothesis as a new orthodoxy. As soon as he alerts us to its possibility, he immediately undercuts it:

> Or maybe they did committ them. Or maybe my mother and father got away with false passports for crimes they didn't committ. How do you spell comit? Of one thing we are sure. Everything is elusive. God is elusive. Revolutionary morality is elusive. Justice is elusive. Human character. Quarters for the cigarette machine. You've got these two people in the poster, Daniel, now how you going to get them out? (42–43)

The only certainty is indeterminacy. The desire for connection is understandable, but one must master his passion for closure if he is to avoid duplicating the crimes of the state in his own perceptions. (Though it may promise to relieve his anguish, Daniel does not pretend to be an omniscient author of the Isaacson case.) Once any account becomes "closed," whether through the pernicious efforts of the State or through sheer familiarity, it threatens to become invisible, unless it is "decreated" and thereby reopened for consideration.[43] Doctorow explains that the consolation for enduring the problem of verifiability is democratic access and influence: "I certainly would much rather trust as a source of truth the variousness of literature, and its width and breadth, than, for instance, a press release from a government agency, or even a sermon. It seems to me what must be maintained is the absolute multiplicity of us all, the numbers of us who color the palette from which the society draws its own portrait."[44] What differentiates the novelist from other wordmongers, says Doctorow, is that he confesses his fabrications to be just that; he does not succumb to his own deceptions. When Doctorow declares that he writes "out of a spirit of transgression,"[45] he is at once renegotiating the borders of the factual and administering the same tactics of incrimination to his own works that he levels at regime mythology and the "appurtenances of theater" upon which its institutions rely (198). ("Probably none of this is true," Daniel confides (249), never relying for long on his metaphors, among which Doctorow's assessment of events of the 1950s in terms of their "amplified" reality during the Viet Nam War era is but the most apparent.) In this spirit, Daniel shows his tolerance for ambiguity in the very form of his book, which does not really conclude but just presents a series of alternative endings (at which point he is 'delivered" from the library during the student takeover of Columbia University). The act of investigation corrupts the object of investigation: that is the Uncertainty Principle of art.

> Daniel's eyes focused on the surface of the windshield, trying to anticipate the small explosions of rain. This was too difficult, so he fixed on one drop and followed its career. The idea was that his attention made it different from the other drops. It arrived, head busted, with one water bead as a nucleus and six or seven clusters in a circle around it. It was like a melted snowflake. Each of the mini-drop clusters combined and became elongated and pulled away in the direction of its own weight. As he accelerated the car, so did they increase their rate of going away from the center. (55)

Facts are mutable, fissionable material, and in the paradoxical phrase of Ronald Sukenick, "Data accumulates obscurity persists."[46] Thus, Daniel's book is submitted "in partial fulfillment of the requirements" only; if the death of his parents is Daniel's *bar mitzvah,* the tentative completion of his narrative is his aesthetic certification. Daniel moves from private injury to a greater spiritual consciousness as he reconnects himself to his family, Lewison to Isaacson, Old Left to New, but *The Book of Daniel* remains a protean, porous work. Daniel may remind us of his father, who "poked his soldering iron into the heart of the radio as if trying to repair the voice" (39) and reprogram history, but his artistic precursor is Poe, who "wore a hole into the parchment and let the darkness pour through" (177).

The undependability of facts in *The Book of Daniel,* not to mention Doctorow's anti-epiphanic "good faith" in resisting both the retreat from contingency and the comfort of a substitute absolute for the absolute he shatters, invites comparison with Walter Abish's depiction of contemporary Germany in *How German Is It*. A meticulously cultivated amnesia conceals the atrocities of World War II; its "rewritten" surface enables Brumholdstein, the novel's setting, to masquerade as one more unremarkable locus of glass-faced buildings, supermarkets, airports, and up-to-date fashions that departicularize, and thus universalize, cities everywhere. In the complacent tone of a travelogue, the novel considers how visitors find the place stripped of intimidating reminders: their attention is first drawn to "the painstaking cleanliness. As well as the all-pervasive sense of order.

A reassuring dependability. A punctuality. An almost obsessive punctuality."[47] E. E. Cummings's condemnation in "pity this busy monster" that "Progress is a comfortable disease" finds its ultimate proof here, in the breezy consumerism that sweeps away the past with the force of ordinance. Like Doctorow's Disneyland, Abish's Germany testifies to the streamlining of history.

Reality seems to have been purged, forced to behave. The new Germany protests its innocence too much, and the conflict between what is seen and what is remembered, between the prepared front and the residual fears, returns us to the novel's title over and over. Does German reality reside in those Dürer equivalents met in face after face in the street? "When one is in Germany and one happens not to be German," we are advised in "The English Garden," Abish's prototype story for the novel, "one is confronted with the problem of determining the relevancy of everything one encounters."[48] So which takes priority: the well-wrought serenity of Brumholdstein, or the Durst deathcamp over which it has been built, and from which reminders occasionally emerge like numerals peeking through sleeves? The soothing blank of a German coloring book, whose version of "the possible . . . will never arouse anyone's disapproval,"[49] contrives a state of affairs that is shaped and sanitized for easy consumption by a public that is largely grateful to be released from their history.

The idols of the new Germany are Egon and Gisela, the modish, prosperous, unreflective representatives of the post-war renaissance. They are idols that require human sacrifices. Although the citizens do reserve a selective reverence for their artists, philosophers, and composers, whatever incriminates is ruled out, "permanently effaced from the world of the coloring book. The faces still awaiting to receive their color show only contentment and pleasure."[50] Abish defines this condition as the security of the familiar, a product of scrupulous care: "The 'familiar' is after all a means of surviving the terror. . . . We do not, it seems, discover the 'familiar' world. We design it, we assemble it."[51] However, the intricacy with which a sense of naturalness is conveyed is what is most unnatural and unsettling to the protagonist of How German Is It, and it initiates suspicion of the "German-ness" of every object, observation, and encounter.

Ulrich Hargenau has much in common with Daniel Isaacson. He too is a writer, and like Doctorow's "little criminal of perception," he "had to admit that writing in some respect was a form of trespassing" (36). Like Daniel he shoulders the burden of a name that creates his identity. Ulrich's father was executed in 1944 for participating in a plot against Hitler, and Ulrich's attempts to "authorize" himself—as a writer, as a German, as a political animal—are in large measure determined by the evolving reputation of his father. The media deem Ulrich's association with the radical Enzieh Group cowardly while praising the "selfless conduct" of the elder Hargenau, diligently formulating the boundaries of acceptability. These manipulations are the spoils of rulership described by Hannah Arendt in *Origins of Totalitarianism*, in which she states that the entrenched power, "independent of all experience," disseminates a "total explanation" that "springs not from lust for power . . . nor for profit . . . but only for ideological reasons: to make the world consistent, to prove that its respective supersense has been right."[52]

A Final Solution is as unsupportable in fiction as it is in human history. But Ulrich himself tends toward the practice of Hayden White's "emplotment" as he indulges in the effort "to view and place his personal affairs in a literary context, as if this would endow them with a clearer and richer meaning" (48). Not only does this habit promise to exculpate him in his dealings with his brother (an architect of the revitalized cityscape), his estranged wife (a member of the Enzieh Group), and his lover (who may have been planted to elicit information from him), it shields him from victimization during the political trials whose script casts him as a scapegoat for terrorist incidents.

Thus, Ulrich becomes a prononent of an unsanctioned reading of history. Despite his protest during an interview that a novel does not rebel against but rather "validates and makes acceptable forms of human conduct" and the institutions they operate within (53), he comes to learn that his work is as threatening to the polished veneer of the new Germany as the serial bombings that interrupt the narrative. Complacency (imaged in *The Book of Daniel* as life in a subway tollbooth) is a betrayal of the writer's craft; or, as the maxim read in *The Book of Daniel*, "The failure to make connections is complicity." History is not just recovered (or re-covered) Germany. It is also the mass grave disclosed by a cave-in; it is also the neuroses of Egon and Gisela that the popular magazines neglect; it is also the ancestral guilt whose memory erodes confidence in contemporary stereotypes. And perhaps most disturbingly, it is also the eruptions of terrorism that periodically ruin "the intrinsic harmony of our society"

(130) by introducing ambiguities, doubts, and anxieties—what Stephen Sloan refers to in *Simulating Terrorism* as unassimilatable signs.[53] The new German citizen may be a political victim of pre-meditated chaos, in which case the random outbreaks are according to plan, or he may be an existential victim of the inherent shapelessness of events, in which case the painted veil—the glossy consumerist sheen of contemporary Germany—is torn away. In any event, the crumbling of familiar contexts opens up streets, text, and consciousness. When the indoctrinated suddenly find themselves *readers,* the result can be panic or intoxication. As Christopher Butler declares, Abish "plays with and subverts our notions of ideology and of an 'order of things' in the world, by refusing to assert mastery over them. This leaves us as readers free to play with interpretation of the comically disoriented world projected by the text."[54]

From another perspective, this is more a matter of obligation than of freedom. While it may be personally expedient to delimit history to satisfy our longings for clarity and composure (and, in the case of *How German Is It,* to absolve people from an indefensible heritage), it is politically and ethically necessary to resist that impulse and instead "reopen the case." By employing a steadfastly "interrogatory style," Abish activates moral energies that compel us to combat "the mind-numbing effect of a static form of representation" on the one hand, and a conditioned sentimentality toward the past on the other: "It is thus in the role of 'artist' that the observer is called upon to discover his own 'art,' which assumes responsibility for his personal deliverance. The author thereby liberates the reader in his capacity as a member of the post-Auschwitz generation from the temptation to cling tenaciously to specific and fixed images of himself in relation to the Nazi pogroms."[55]

For Abish, art is no analgesic, nor history a burial. Defamiliarization is a mandatory precedent to honest historical inquiry. It demolishes the pretense of the placid travelogue style of the book and interrupts the pleasant drowse of the contemporary population. It opposes the abstruse meditations of Brumhold, the philosopher for whom the city was named, whose thinking deflects the issue of his country's past; it opposes the moral lassitude of Helmuth Hargenau, the architect who "bulldozes the past as if it never occurred."[56] On the contrary, Ulrich must acknowledge the past—his and Germany's—if he is ever going to *move.* This may be the symbolic lesson of the miniature replica of the Durst concentration camp that a local waiter is putting together in his basement: "What he was doing was to evoke in the people he knew a sense of uncertainty, a sense of doubt, a sense of dismay, a sense of disgust" (158). Underground movements threaten "the reciprocity of perfections" that constitute the new German myth, whose basis, according to Egon, is "the craving to attain a total harmony" (127, 131). Totality, harmony, completion—these are the insidious rewards of complicity that the conscientious artist-historian must avoid.

So it is that the concluding scene of the novel finds Ulrich undergoing hypnotic treatment to confirm his discovery that he is not the son of his executed namesake. (As it was for Daniel, for Ulrich the contentment of reliable parentage is yet one more casualty of analysis.) He awakens from a trance to see himself holding his right hand aloft in a Nazi salute. "Is it possible for anyone in Germany, nowadays, to raise his right hand, for whatever the reason, and not be flooded by the memory of a dream to end all dreams?" (252). Ulrich accepts the duty to embrace all implications and thereby separates himself from the general rush to oblivion that surrounds him—the purged surface of the coloring book.

How German Is It is deeply concerned with the degree to which language itself leads us away from such confrontations because it is a fundamental guarantor of familiarity. Helmuth, Ulrich's brother, champions his native language for its precision, richness, and adaptability to the construction of a new society; but inherent in the German tongue, argues George Steiner in "The Hollow Miracle," are the horrifying memories of the Nazi past. "Nazism found in the language precisely what it needed to give voice to its savagery," he claims. "Hitler heard inside his native tongue the latent hysteria, the confusion, the quality of hypnotic trance. He plunged unerringly into the undergrowth of language, into those zones of darkness and outcry. . . . He sensed in German another music than that of Goethe, Heine, and Mann; a rasping cadence, half nebulous jargon, half obscenity."[57] In this sense, language itself exhibits the historical layering of cities and citizens.

Beneath the organized march of words is a network of troubling relations; the alternative, no less threatening, is an abyss of irreconcilability, in which all data are discrete, atomized. "What is most monstrous is sequence," Daniel confides in *The Book of Daniel* (245), not only because it subjects the analyst to distracting patterns but because it coaxes him into accepting those patterns as insights by neatly compensating his attempts at judgment. Either extreme—total connectedness or utter disconnection—is deadly; in *The Book of Daniel,* it can be witnessed in Daniel's meditation between the impasses represented by Susan's self-interment as a "starfish" and the Inertia Kid's unmooring, with heart, eyes, tongue, and limbs "lying in their own slackened strings."[58]

Don DeLillo's *The Names* focuses on this strain between the psychological enchantments of pattern—whether abiding superstructure or overriding conspiracy—and the suspicion of pattern as played out against the backdrop of international corporate intrigue. James Axton works for the Northeast Group, a shadowy multinational conglomerate with possible CIA connections, as a "risk analyst," calculating the advisability of investment against the volatility of developing nations in which investments are situated. The book is populated by modern corporate nomads, political terrorists, and religious zealots whose cryptic ventures are played out against the backdrop of the "polyglot surge" of languages, alphabets, and codes.[59] Ranging from Greece to the Middle East to India, *The Names* internationalizes the concerns of *The Book of Daniel* and intensifies the problem raised in *How German Is It* of how crises of historical intelligibility distill into a general crisis of illegibility: all the characters in the novel are lexical traffickers in a semiotic universe.

The catalog of Adamic impulses and practices in *The Names* is enormous. Everyone is an etymologist of sorts; everyone must steer through a surfeit of argots, interpreting and producing language, for language—the act of naming—is at once a stay against the unassimilatable flow of contemporary reality and a perpetuation of its mystery. The collision of alphabets and intimacies in the novel seems almost endless. There are the amenities of political protocol and the swirl of corporate jargon, replete with telexes, memoranda, and clandestine deals. There is the mute eloquence of inscriptions and runes unearthed by Owen Brademas, a director of archaeological excavations and professional "epigrapher," for whom stones speak and whose ongoing fascination with "the geography of language" (35) carries beyond deciphering the fallout of lost cultures to an obsession with the architecture of alphabets, those enduring extensions of the self. There are the statistics of risk analysis and the rarefied symmetries of pure mathematics. There are the Braille textures of landscapes, whose "semantic rudiments" (180) press upon Axton's consciousness with their pregnant geometry. The novel is rich with tongues, including such private codes as Ob (a pig-Latin used by Axton's precocious son, Tap, who is himself composing a novel based on Brademas) and *boustrophedon* (an ancient writing style based upon the formal movement of oxen in the field). There are the surreptitious transactions of the CIA, itself a cult of vague practices and practiced vagaries to which Axton eventually discovers his own organization is closely allied. There are marital sharings and adulteries, flirtations, sexual double entendres, body languages (including an expressive bellydance by a bored wife)—all the trappings of human connection, "the conscious hovering sum of things" (123). There are rituals and customs, cults and vendettas, furtive graffiti and esoterica, liaisons and subterfuges, all that scrupulous inwardness, epitomized perhaps by the mysteries of myth, the messianic activities of religious fanatics, and the Koranic ninety-nine names of God, who is "the river of language" (152).

At the beginning of the novel, Axton is eager to insulate himself as best he can from all of these "streams of belief" (146) and insistent patterns and purposes, so he adopts an air of preoccupation, skepticism, and resolute distance. What eventually beguiles him, however, is one particular pattern: an eerie cult, The Names, has been murdering people who have apparently been singled out according to the matching up of their initials with those of the place where the brutal killings (their heads are crushed by hammer blows) occur. The cultists are abecedarian activists, structural terrorists. "The possibility is haunting," thinks Axton, "that there is an exact correspondence at the center of all this confusion, this formlessness of motive and plan and execution. A harmony" (327). DeLillo's narrator is reminiscent of Pynchon's system-detectives Oedipa Maas, who is seduced and subsumed by the W.A.S.T.E. underground in *The Crying of Lot 49*, and Herbert Stencil, who vainly labors to contain the multiplicitous forms of *V.*, yet who finds modern history "rippled with gathers in its fabric such that if we are situated, as Stencil seemed to be, at the bottom of a fold, it's impossible to determine warp, woof or pattern anywhere else."[60] A writer and researcher like Daniel Isaacson and Ulrich Hargenau, James Axton brings the tactics and temperament of an intelligence agent to bear upon the systematic outrages of The Names; again, like Pynchon's Stencil, he tries to manufacture continuity out of a "grand Gothic pile of inferences."[61] But his awakened interrogative spirit is frustrated. Intelligence strategies, after all, are founded upon a faith in intelligibility, and the world resists that striving toward interpretive closure; or, as the lesson is put in another of DeLillo's novels, analysis eventually runs aground against "the screech and claw of the inexpressible."[62]

Adrift among "the ornaments of paranoia and deception" (44), Axton reaches an impasse which is as much linguistic as it is political. Saturated with writings, *The Names* does not finally dissolve their essential opacity. The cult killings are the gruesome signature of unfathomable minds; neither the confessions of a renegade cultist nor the diplomatic forays of Frank Volterra, the experimental director who desires to capture and promote the cult on film, do much to dispel the essential obscurity of their motives. The more he uncovers, the more Axton feels besieged by the "grim, inexplicable universe":

> There was around us almost nothing we knew as familiar and safe. Only our hotels rising from the lees of perennial renovation. The sense of things was different in such a way that we could only register the edges of some elaborate secret. It seemed we'd lost our capacity to select, to ferret out particularity and trace it to some center which our minds could relocate in knowable surroundings. There was no equivalent core. The forces were different, the orders of response eluded us. Tenses and inflections. Truth was different, the spoken universe, and men with guns were everywhere. (94)

The avalanche of data, the burgeoning panorama of human events, the chaos of contingency and suspicion: Axton is "overwhelmed by the powerful rush of things, the raw proximity and lack of common measure" (280) against which reductive interrogations—the trappings of "linguistic arrogance"—prove futile (240). It is instructive that the password of The Names is "How many languages do you speak?" The mind, by nature bureaucratic and fastidious and raging for order, may struggle to refine and contain these jarring, byzantine surfaces—James Axton opens his narrative by describing the modern city of Athens as featureless, irreconcilable, hissing, blaring—but in the end there is no gathering those intricate ravels into some perfect, "sculpted hush" (8). Axton faces the dilemma of Hayden White's historian who urges data to "conform to an icon of a comprehensible finished process," even as his sophistries confirm and aggravate "the opaqueness of the world" he confronts:

> Each new historical work only adds to the number of possible texts that have to be interpreted if a full and accurate picture of a given historical milieu is to be faithfully drawn. The relationship between the past to be analyzed and historical works produced by analysis of the documents is paradoxical; the more we know about the past, the more difficult it is to generalize about it.[63]

No single configuration will produce a conclusive "harmony." As Louis O. Mink maintains, although "narrative histories should be aggregative, insofar as they are histories," they "cannot be, insofar as they are narratives," which result in the generation of imaginative spaces that defy consolidation.[64]

An antidote to Stencil-like preoccupations in *The Names* is provided by Axton's son, Tap, whose novel-in-progress celebrates Owen Brademas, an eager reader of the world with a special gift for "yielding" to things. *The Names* chronicles Axton's progress toward the same sort of receptive sensibilities; he must undergo "an evolution of seeing" (179). If Axton begins as a latter-day Ahab hoping to "strike through the mask"—the massive, glyphic head of Moby-Dick serves as a model for the looming, peremptory Parthenon whose image opens DeLillo's novel—he ends by supplanting his narrative with Tap's, in which it is a curse to be tongue-tied in a word-soaked world. "White words . . . Pure as the drivelin snow" (336) respect the marvelous.

The Names adds to the dilemma of relating versus creating history by emphasizing throughout the book the distrust of the medium upon which the historian must rely to develop and express a fluid reality. As Emmerich, a member of The Names, confides to Owen Brademas, a weapon branded with the owner's name in runic letters "is not history. This is precisely the opposite of history. An alphabet of utter stillness. We track static letters when we read. This is a logical paradox" (291–92). Roland Barthes' suspicion of the explanatory capacities of history is relevant here as well, in that as a product of linguistic engineering, history enjoys no special pre-eminence; indeed, a given history first and foremost depicts its historian by manifesting his craft, his goals, his penchants and idiosyncrasies as he seeks to abstract and tailor the world's density to his needs.

The impact of the discovery of The Names compares with that of the enigmatic message from space in *Ratner's Star* and the "airborne toxic event" in *White Noise:* the lives of DeLillo's protagonists are thrust savagely into relief by phenomena that overpower their psychic "stabilizers." The victory reached by James Axton does not depend upon his solving a terrorist riddle or some government's grammar but upon his repudiation of static formulas in favor of the creative fluidity of life and language: "We must be equal to the largeness of things" (89). Axton's resigning his job with the Northeast Group to return to "freelancing" coincides with Daniel Isaacson's stand against "regime language." In effect, the activities of the intelligence agency and those of the cult of murderers are alike in their brutal superimposition of determinate systems upon a mutable reality; and in the end, Axton "seeks expression, connection, and satisfaction through language, not repression of individuality in exchange for false security."[65] In the end, too, he is ready to appreciate the "muddy" writings of Tap as inspiring, bursting with optimistic energy and the promise of dissolving the congestion of stock responses. "I found these mangled words exhilarating. He'd made them new again, made me see how they worked, what they really were. They were ancient things, secret, reshapable" (313). Ambiguity is not denounced as impasse but championed as potential.

In his essay "Not-Knowing," Donald Barthelme announces that the writer relies upon a creed of open-endedness that entitles him to options yet to be disclosed: "the writer is a man who, embarking upon a task, does not know what to do."[66] His is a discursive mentality, not a subjugating one. At the beginning of *The Names,* Axton's renunciation just leaves him pinched and sullen. Axton's subsequent discoveries about himself and the world he occupies ventilate the imagination even as they qualify its products. So we rush to coin oxymorons that refute "subdue and codify" logic: fruitful indecisiveness, rich confusion, "ambitious uncertainty."[67]

James Axton concludes his tale by describing his pilgrimage to the Parthenon, whose aloofness and brooding ambiguity had always proved so daunting to him: "I move past the scaffolding and walk down the steps, hearing one language after another, rich, harsh, mysterious, strong. This is what we bring to the temple, not prayer or chant or slaughtered rams. Our offering is language" (331). In this way, Axton matures into an artist like DeLillo himself, who extols the opportunity afforded the writer "to shape himself as a human being through the language he uses. I think written language, fiction, goes that deep. He not only sees himself but begins to make himself or remake himself. Of course, this is mysterious and subjective territory."[68]

Having resigned his position with the Northeast Group to freelance write again—the term itself connotes liberation and receptivity—Axton accepts a fragmented, tentative technique. Appropriately, *The Names* joins *The Book of Daniel* by refusing to choke off possibilities: Daniel's multiple endings to his inquiry find their counterpart in the in-progress affirmation of openness and open-endedness of Tap's writing. Tap's hero does not arrive at some totalizing terminus, but rather remains in flux, inchoate and wondering. "Thus, instead of a tidy, hence crippling conclusion, the reader is allowed to share the characters' mingled relish and trepidation as they anticipate and move toward a new, perhaps satisfying personal contact with language."[69] We need only recall the redefinition of the image of the Parthenon at the conclusion of *The Names* to appreciate the "shimmering" quality of DeLillo's novel: what began as an imperious, impregnable threat has now become elastic, inviting, and containing an "open cry" of "human feeling" that is "deeper than the art and mathematics embodied in the structure, the optical exactitudes" (330). Whereas Virginia Woolf's Lily Briscoe, an exemplary modern artist, reached a finished vision at the end of *To the Lighthouse,* James Axton learns the futility of trying to coerce such closure from life or from language. Epistemology focuses on the dynamics of questions rather than on the final domestication of answers.

In his review of Charles Newman's *The Post-Modern Aura,* Ihab Hassan cautions against nostalgia for:

> a transparent history, altogether unproblematic, that fully reveals its meaning to the beholder, should he but turn back his head. . . . It is also a pacified history, oblivious of otherness, difference, quiddity, of everything that resists recovery, use, assimilation. It is, clearly, history as unambiguous authority, a power that *answers,* sanctions, legitimates amid all our delegitimations.[70]

That so unskeptical a model of history ever held sway is questionable at best. Surely, the conception of history that presides over contemporary fiction defies consistency or consensus, and it is the malleability of the past that makes it simultaneously frustrating and inviting to creative sensibilities like those enlisted above. With reality's record a matter of the reach of personal eloquence, a narrator like legal consort Marcus Gorman, for instance, can recast our memory of the murdered gangster Jack "Legs" Diamond as a pioneering combination of Horatio Alger, Finn McCool, and Jesse James:

> He advanced the cause of joyful corruption and vice. He put the drop of the creature on the parched tongues of millions. He filled the pipes that pacify the troubled, loaded the needles that puncture anxiety bubbles. He helped the world kick the gong around, Jack did. And was he thanked for his benevolence? Hardly. The final historical image that endures is that corpse clad in underwear, flat-assed out in bed, broke and alone.[71]

As self-appointed oracle of a more appealing myth, William Kennedy's Gorman redeems the past to pad his own ego, borrowing vicariously from his subject "a little Gargantuan dimension."[72]

A chapter title from John Barth's *The Sot-Weed Factor* emphasizes the intricate, and ultimately insufficient, apparatus that the imagination brings to the fore: "The Poet Wonders Whether The Course of Human History Is a Progress, A Drama, a Retrogression, a Cycle, an Undulation, a Vortex, a Right- or Left-Handed Spiral, a Mere Continuum, or What Have You. Certain Evidence Is Brought Forward, but of an Ambiguous and Inconclusive Nature."[73] Narrative mounts and records the process of its appropriations; experience stimulates expression without finally conforming to its strictures. The artist of history refuses both oversimplification and exile. He rigs insights in the shadow of indeterminacies that afford his creations consequence without tenure.

Chapter 4

De(in)forming the Plot

> 5. In the further development of the story, would you like
> more emotion ( ) or less emotion ( )?
> 6. Is there too much *blague* in the narration? ( ) Not
> enough *blague*? ( )
> 7. Do you feel that the creation of new modes of hysteria is a
> viable undertaking for the artist of today? Yes ( ) No ( )
> 8. Would you like a war? Yes ( ) No ( )
> 9. Has the work, for you, a metaphysical dimension? Yes ( )
> No ( )
> 10. What is it (twenty-five words or less)?
>
> —from *Snow White,* by Donald Barthelme

As epiphanic potential diminishes and the prospects for closure either collapse into impasses or evaporate into indeterminacies, traditional fictional formulas are summoned to account. Because they imply reliable, explicit avenues for the reader to travel on the way to resolutions that contemporary fiction reneges on, conventional models of coherence and plot development cannot be recovered intact from literary history. Nevertheless, the tendency to be examined in this chapter is not to dismiss these formulas as obsolete, but rather to invoke them for purposes of parody—to employ them in order to subvert them. Stories of detection and quest, emblems of the search-and-seizure mentality of the revelational plot (or, more aptly, plotted revelation) have been redesigned in contemporary fiction to conform to a modesty of aims enforced by an irremediably cryptic world. In each case that follows, the assumption of progressive insight under which the narrative formula ordinarily operates is sabotaged; consequently, the structural components of the ordering imagination—story lines cultivated over centuries of use—are openly interrogated on the page.

That authors persist in importing narrative formulas that arouse their skepticism reveals their nostalgia for the promise of integration they contain; the other side of parody is pining for fictional procedures that have ceased to abide. Roland Barthes has insisted that "the very end of myths is to immobilize the world; they must suggest and mimic a universal order,"[1] which suggests that the fixities of myth are ultimately transferable to other realms of human endeavor. However, contemporary fiction resists the anthropomorphic alchemy that would allow these formulas to function with impunity. The inductive arsenals upon which generations of detectives relied provide no remedy; the heirs of gallant questors dissolve into randomness or never get under way at all, their tales caught in the door; while artists once were heroes of their own making, able to mobilize words in confirmation of their calling, now there is no pregnant gesture, no reckless flashing or measured surge. Their common legacy is an indefinite flux, a derailed dream of the self-under-construction. In *The Sense of an Ending*, Frank Kermode describes how fictions serve as models of time and destiny, providing "fictive concords" that systematize existence and wring consonance from its flow.[2] But the contemporary novel tends to expand and exploit the gap of deferral between origins and conclusions. Fiction has become an ellipsis stretched story-wide.

At the core of this condition lies the abolition of the concept of character as a viable entity. Bulletins from such formidable petitioners as D. H. Lawrence protesting that we would seek in vain "the old stable ego of the character" in his work, and from Virginia Woolf that human character had changed irrevocably "in or about December, 1910" laid claim to broader provinces of consciousness and psychological complexity in the depiction of character in fiction.[3] Subsequent challenges to those conventions, on the other hand, have opposed, and in many instances reversed, the sophistication of character evidenced by the Modernists. The contemporary novel tends to feature a decadent hero, shriveled beyond humanistic sympathies, even beyond recognition. Raymond Federman heralds a version of character as little more than a bit of verbal fallout in the midst of deliberately incoherent, incorrigibly playful texts: "The creatures of the new fiction will be as changeable, as unstable, as illusory, as nameless, as unnamable, as fraudulent, as unpredictable as the discourse that makes them."[4] Wylie Sypher insists that the romantic notion of independent selfhood has been effaced from the twentieth century, and it has been replaced by the "defensive humanism" of modern art that more appropriately reflects our status as anonymous "functionaries" robbed of centrality.[5] William Gass goes so far as to maintain that a character is fundamentally, quite literally, a body of words: "the noise of his name" surrounded by "empty space and silence," or indeed, broadening the compass, any locus in fiction to which attention attaches, from an idea or an event to "a stone in a stream or that soap in Bloom's pocket."[6]

In short, characters can be so amorphous or so promiscuous that it is often difficult to keep them pinned and wriggling in the mind with the old-fashioned referential arrows of mimetic theory. The carefully outlined, discrete, and dependable citizens of the text have melted into fluid processes that require the mutual, ongoing interaction of author, text, and reader to shape into temporary sense, as witnessed in Ronald Sukenick's *Out* when "Roland Sycamore you don't know this yet peeled off from the Sukenick character after the karate fight and the latter is no longer a character at all but the real me if that's possible."[7] At the other extreme from the rebellion of character against the subjugation of the proper noun strapped to him is the self collapsed into a period, a mote borne along by the text. This is the sort of character that cultural anatomists like Christopher Lasch maintain to be the product of a narcissistic culture, "which reveals itself in a pervasive despair of understanding the course of modern history or of subjecting it to rational direction,"[8] and in which all of our energies, or such that remain to us in an environment of minimized aspirations and minimal gains, are centripetal. In the words of John Ashbery in his poem "The Wrong Kind of Insurance," "We straggle on as quotients, hard-to-combine / Ingredients."[9]

If the self must perform as a subjective presence in the world—the embodiment of viewpoint, index of purpose, or authenticating weight—in order for traditional plot formulas to function successfully, the "voided" characters under discussion do not have sufficient selves to posit. James Purdy's incurious seekers, Ronald Sukenick's stream-of-character voices, and Thomas Pynchon's comically stripped cartoons barely leave a trace of personality, much less marshal a vigorous ego or investigative drive.

Furthermore, if characters cannot achieve the mandatory focus to address the world, neither does the world welcome their advances. Contemporary fiction largely dispenses with the hospitable "forest of symbols" that greeted the Transcendentalists, and instead laments the irreducible alienness of whatever lurks "out there." As Gabriel Josipovici argues, whereas once analogies offered access to eternal verities, the "demonic analogies" of the present betray us, leaving us with "the feeling that what we had taken to be 'the world' is only the projection of our private compulsions: *analogy* becomes a sign of *dementia*."[10] Oedipa Maas's harried considerations in *The Crying of Lot 49* are now customary:

> Either way, they'll call it paranoia. They. Either you have stumbled indeed, without the aid of LSD or other indole alkaloids, onto a secret richness and concealed density of dream; . . . Or you are hallucinating it. Or a plot has been

mounted against you, . . . Or you are fantasying some such plot, in which case you are a nut, Oedipa, out of your skull.[11]

Oedipa's consolation in the face of labyrinthine conspiracy is that intricacy implies calculation and purpose. But the novel unfolds merely to expose more folds. Fiction must compromise its belief in empirical logic, analytical consistency, and common sense in view of the "unreal" realities that proliferate around it. Accordingly, Josipovici maintains that art has been reassigned from serving as the key to the universe to exposing the essential uniqueness of each of its contents, to the exclusion of any encompassing explanation.[12] Or, as Alain Robbe-Grillet announces, "Around us, defying the noisy pack of our animistic or protective adjectives, things *are* there. . . . All our literature has not yet succeeded in eroding their smallest corner, their slightest curve."[13] Reality refuses to comply with our humanizing assaults upon it, and what we call the absurdity of the human condition is the impossibility of a "final recuperation of all distances, of all failures, of all solitudes, of all contradictions."[14] The fate of fictional plots that survive this erosion of confidence is self-conscious decomposition.

The mythic injunctions of the detective novel, for example, are that experience is marked out and determinable, contrived in such a way as to reward efforts of ratiocination; motive begets crime, and effects can be tracked to their causes like bloodstains to a wound. The detective himself is a hero of logic, for whom awareness is a matter of steady accumulation of clues and patient execution of analytical talents. His is the smug, "just-the-facts-ma'am" mindset of Dickens's Gradgrind or television's Joe Friday, whose clubby confidence radiates from what Thomas Pynchon facetiously calls "the stone determinacy of everything."[15] In writing about the profound psychological consolations of detective fiction, C. Day Lewis goes so far as to propose that the aura of faith it furnishes suggests a modern substitute for religion, as he envisions some future cultural historian noting:

> a significant parallel between the formalized denouement of the detective novel and the Christian conception of the Day of Judgement, when with a flourish of trumpets, the mystery is made plain and the goats are separated from the sheep.[16]

But contemporary versions of the genre admit accidents and gaps, loose and dead ends, for their world is immune to translation. Whereas the puzzles posed by conventional detective novels are recontextualized at some delayed, yet dependable, last-minute appointment in the story, anti-epiphanic examples of the genre dwell upon the linguistic foundation of knowledge and remain as suspicious of solutions as of the problems that occasion them.[17] Objects of scrutiny become elements in imaginative distortion; events are storified by detectives whose anxious approximations do not resemble science so much as they do art. And as their self-consciousness over their activities grows more acute, as the framework upon which the detective's code of honor and his hypothesizing abilities rely is subjected to the likelihood that all patterning is expedient, not absolute, the detective novel feasts on its own verbal processes.

This is particularly true of Paul Auster's New York Trilogy: *City of Glass, Ghosts,* and *The Locked Room,*[18] each of which features a private eye focused inward on the "private I," and each of which reassigns the detective out of his traditional investigations and into epistemological errands and metafictional tangles.

The Chinese-box effect of *City of Glass* enforces these "vertical" concerns at the expense of the horizontal plot surge that is typical of the detective formula. Paul Auster, the novel's author, presents us with his hero, Quinn, who is also a mystery novelist and who publishes under the pseudonym of William Wilson, whose fictional hero is named Max Work, a hard-boiled detective of the Dashiell Hammett/Raymond Chandler school. As a result of a wrong number, Quinn is mistaken by a mysterious caller for one Paul Auster, who runs a detective agency; in fact, of course, Paul Auster the novelist is the "agency" from which the stratified characters of *City of Glass* derive. Thus, a sort of identity relay system is established on the glassy surface of the novel; like the surfictions of Federman and Sukenick, *City of Glass* exchanges a hierarchy of realistic depths for a surface of interpenetrating planes of equivalent credibility, all flattened out by, and as, language. The realist's mirror in the road has become the deflecting nature of all reality, much like the smooth, gleaming surfaces of the skyscrapers of New York: "The question is the story itself," we are warned at the outset, "and whether or not it means something is not for the story to tell" (7).

Acquiescence to the inevitability of mystery pervades the novel and short-circuits the operations of the detective. Causal chains are refuted as mere artifacts of an anxious imagination; the business of data-gathering is dismissed as ultimately useless—there are no such things as vital statistics because motives are impenetrable, relationships opaque. Quinn surrenders himself to aimlessness; he drifts in whatever direction accident sweeps him along. The acquisition of experience simply increases his feeling of lostness "not only in the city, but within himself as well" (8), so that Quinn is little more than a self-confessed floating integer in textual space, a parody of Emerson's transparent eyeball who bloats himself on the Void: "And this, finally, was all he ever asked of things: to be nowhere. New York was the nowhere he had built around himself, and he realized that he had no intention of ever leaving it again" (9).

Quinn's ready acceptance of the role in which the wrong number casts him is consistent with his writer's reliance on pseudonyms and alter egos, which he welcomes as opportunities to escape himself. Like John Barth's Jacob Horner in *The End of the Road,* Quinn would otherwise be marooned in a state of "weatherlessness" were he not available to the "mythotherapeutic" adoption of a variety of guises, complete with relevant argots, actions, and gestures that relieve him of the responsibility to improvise an authentic self on his own. As an accomplished trafficker in the world of detective fiction, Quinn is compelled by the opportunity to base himself on his work (and on his Max Work) that the telephone call from Virginia Stillman provides. (We may recall how relieved Huck Finn was to learn that the role expected of him at the Phelps farm was a familiar one—Tom Sawyer—which he had been trying to enact for some time anyway.) Significantly, Quinn takes the case on the anniversary of the day he was conceived, which he now celebrates as his birthday, and to be sure, he is conceived as a character at the instant that he is summoned onto the stage of events. The appropriated Auster identity, upholstered by Quinn's own Max Work, is a dream of prowess and efficiency he can enter; the appointment with Virginia Stillman, much like Vladimir and Estragon's appointment with Godot, holds out the promise of substance. Quinn, until now a character like an unmade bed, whose empty solitude better depicted a deprived I than a private eye, is found and founded by the phone call—it stands for the annunciation and the enunciation of the formerly unspecified self.

Unfortunately, in contrast to the "crisp assurances" of Marco Polo in his *Travels,* which Quinn reads for leisure and confidence, the case that Quinn has embarked upon defies translation. He is seized by doubt and arbitrariness, and instead of rousing him out of automatism, the "call" places him in a trance: "I seem to be going out"; "I seem to have arrived"; "If all this is really happening." Quinn suffers a dissociation of sensibilities that starkly contrasts with the sober progress towards omniscience that is the privilege of the hardboiled detective, for whom facts submit to the universal solvent of hypothesis. Once again, William V. Spanos provides the relevant analysis of postmodern disenfranchisement. The aim of coercive Western structures of consciousness, spurred by positivistic zeal, is to reorient fugitive clues and fragments beneath "the vantage point of a final rational cause." However, Spanos explains, the transcendent equilibrium that might solve the "'crime' of contingent existence" is at a premium beyond the means of the contemporary hero.[19] Certainty hovers, then disperses; fact after blurry fact eludes assimilation.

The case itself is a protracted version of the anxious queries of Beckett's Unnamable: "Where now? Who now?" Peter Stillman is in need of protection from his father, a draconian professor of theology who had once subjected his son to a macabre experiment that required his being locked in a dark room for nine years, until a sudden fire led to the boy's being hospitalized (he would later marry his speech therapist, Virginia) and Stillman's being remanded to an insane asylum. Now that the elder Stillman is being released, Virginia is anxious to have him tailed. But Peter, who oscillates between wordless stupor and manic volubility, is a fitful spectre, a verbal spastic: his confessions are half-parable, half-gibberish, and the words he can muster fly about like wild birds. An amnesiac witness to his own experiences, Peter is still a captive of darkness, the victim of a crazed, glowering god. Taking his testimony is like glossing a blank, for Peter, prelinguistic and at bay, embodies T. S. Eliot's dilemma in *East Coker:* "Trying to learn to use words, and every attempt/Is a wholly new start, and a different kind of failure."[20] Thus, Virginia's eager flattery of Quinn—she calls him "the answer" and "the right man" (50)—is doubly mistaken because not only is he impersonating the detective she had hoped to engage, but all of his attempts at inference—at placing a tail/tale on Stillman—disintegrate. Frustrations mount, as untrustworthy accounts, parallels in literature (Quinn ruminates about other "wild child" episodes in *Robinson Crusoe* and *Kaspar Hauser*), Quinn's remorse over the death of his own child (who was also named Peter), and teasingly allegorical names cluster about the case. Not even a photograph of Stillman sparks any insight in Quinn: in fact, it is so old that Quinn worries whether or not he will be able to recognize the man he is supposed to track.

Stillman's research into the relationship between man's spiritual and linguistic Falls, as detailed in excerpts from his book debating the nature of pre-civilized man, provokes a host of analogies to the detective novel itself. Stillman sought to purify his son's language—to restore severed language to intimacy with God—by removing Peter from the contaminated, post-lapsarian matrix of worldly reality, whose dubious foundation is the Tower of Babel. His discovery of the (apocryphal?) efforts of Henry Dark, amanuensis of the great cosmographer John Milton, to reverse the Fall by recuperating the innocent language of Eden had obsessed Stillman to the extent that he forced the project on his son. However, like the building of the Tower of Babel itself, this experiment may have been more hubristic than worshipful, as evidenced perhaps by its tragic results. Were the American Indians studied by Stillman beneficiaries of utopian grace or the unregenerate victims of spiritual neglect? Was the Biblical exegesis of Dark a prophetic insight or a lie of poetry? An access to a world purged of words or an entrapment by words?

Similarly, Quinn, already consumed by the memory of his son's fatal fall, cannot trust the associative empire he is building out of these strange details. He tries to adhere to a creed of "clean," unreflective duty—"I have not been hired to understand—merely to act. This is something new. To keep it in mind, at all costs" (65)—but despite his ceremonies of new birth and undistracted embarkation (purchasing a new notebook, clearing the debris from his desk, writing in the nude), there is no disregarding the pressing identifications with the subject of his surveillance. Both Quinn and Stillman, after all, were spawned at the authorial Paul Auster-level of the identity hierarchy, and the whole episode often threatens to unmask itself as an elaborate displacement engineered by a clever mystery writer. Moreover, Quinn's following after Stillman—or rather, his following after one of the two men resembling the photograph whom Quinn selects as his prey as they simultaneously emerge from the train—is also a search for himself, another dispossessed father of a boy named Peter. The absurd dance of detective and detected in *City of Glass* parallels that of Beckett's *Molloy,* in which agent Moran is first professionally, then psychologically, and finally physically absorbed by Molloy. As his mission disintegrates into arbitrariness, Moran learns that coming too close to Molloy (like Stillman, a sort of walking lacuna) exiles him from the brisk certainties of selfhood, and this enterprise leaves such "deep lesions" in his identity that he becomes unrecognizable to himself outside of his imitations of the actions and eccentricities of the man he is merging into.[21]

The detective's capacity for polytropic guile and the novelist's privilege of ventriloquism through his characters only accelerate the "leakage" of Beckett's and Auster's respective protagonists. What had begun as a vacation from self-consciousness and inanition for Quinn (the adoption of the Auster persona) becomes a full-blown identity crisis. Stranded on the threshold of knowing, Quinn fiddles with plots and counterplots not with the manipulative finesse of a Sam Spade but with the furtiveness of a criminal on the lam. "For example: who are you," he writes in his journal. "And if you think you know, why do you keep lying about it? I have no answer. All I can say is this: listen to me. My name is Paul Auster. That is not my real name" (66). The closing lines of *Molloy* set the pattern for this riddle:

> Does this mean I am freer now than I was? I do not know. I shall learn. Then I went back into the house and wrote, It is midnight. The rain is beating on the windows. It was not midnight. It was not raining.[22]

His adopted identity does not enable Quinn to achieve any significant breakthrough—the anonymous constellations cover the sky in cosmic mockery of his failure to "name" his experience (82–83). His surveillance activities are no less susceptible to vagueness, as exemplified by his personal version of the Heisenberg Uncertainty Principle whereby he cannot follow Stillman and take notes simultaneously without losing track of him or producing an illegible text (99–100). Matching his routines, notetaking habits, and even his gait to Stillman's, Quinn finds himself becoming indistinguishable from his subject (recalling Moran's melding into Molloy in Beckett's novel). Stillman's wanderings constitute a patterned aimlessness, a predictable randomness—the precision of the mad. Quinn's efforts to assign purpose to them are chiefly efforts to validate his own expenditure of time and energy. But the more he observes, the more impenetrable Stillman seems to become: "Instead of narrowing the distance that lay between him and Stillman, he had seen the old man slip away from him, even as he remained before his eyes" (105).

Stillman's zombie-like scavenging parallels the verbal cataloguing projects in Gangemi's *OLT*. Quinn maps out Stillman's peregrinations: do they form a rectangle? a circle? an empty zero? Or are they letters inscribed upon the oversized page of New York City? That Quinn ransacks his notes "for some glimmer of cogency" (109) although it may come at the expense of coolly objective principles of detection demonstrates how far he has drifted from the model of his own Max Work; but there it is, whether by accident or intention, foisted or found: TOWER OF BABEL. True enough, Stillman could have known that he was being tailed, in which case he may have been coaxing Quinn into a contrived revelation; it is just as likely, of course, that Quinn has made his own message as a child discovers pictures in the clouds, which would make Quinn, like the compulsive engineers of the Tower of Babel itself, a victim of his own abstraction.

When Quinn finally accosts Stillman, introducing himself as Quinn (now a disguise for the Auster identity, but a confession of sorts from his own perspective), Stillman improvises on his name, as though to assert his control over him. Intriguingly, because words and referents do not cohere for Stillman, each subsequent meeting with Quinn (who employs a new alias each time, including the name Peter Stillman) is a pristine, unprecedented experience. Even so, by defining Quinn as a character in his own book, Stillman retains the upper hand over his anxious interrogator. Stillman confides his semiotic mission to Quinn: to fashion a new language, one that is intrepid, precise, stoutly referential, and equal to the task of contending with our fragmented, post-Babel world. Thanks to his visionary dedication, or to some blown cerebral cylinder, Stillman depicts himself as the Adam of the modern city, an urban disciple of Lewis Carroll's Humpty Dumpty, who wishes to master words, not be mastered by them (127).

Quinn's crisis reaches its climax when he loses track of Stillman. He locates the "real" Paul Auster, the man whom he has been masquerading as, but Auster is no detective either, just a writer like Quinn. Because writers are of no help in solving enigmas—their abilities are restricted to introducing them—Quinn despairs. Auster tries to console the distraught stranger by sharing details of his speculative work-in-progress on the truth-status of the authorship of *Don Quixote*, which reminds us of the Jorge Luis Borges tale "Pierre Menard, Author of the Quixote," as well as recapitulates, in the confusing relationship between the "mad" Quixote and his chronicler, the ambiguous interdependency of Stillman and Quinn. Moreover, Auster's wife and child complete a scene of domestic serenity that Quinn has lost; to be sure, Quinn would have liked to impersonate Auster beyond the shaky pretense he has been maintaining.

By now, Quinn has lost his grip. He wanders about town, taking notes among the ravaged street people from whom he can barely differentiate himself. Ultimately, Quinn resigns himself to a purgatorial life-in-waiting, spying for months from the alley on his clients, suffering self-imposed deprivations of food, shelter, sleep, and company as though enduring penance. The result of this maniacal program is losing himself so completely that he barely feels the loss:

> Now, as he looked at himself in the shop mirror, he was neither shocked nor disappointed. . . . Yes, it seemed more than likely that this was Quinn. Even now, however, he was not upset. The transformation in his appearance had been so drastic that he could not help but be fascinated by it. He had turned into a bum. (182–83)

His vigilance has been so exclusive, so claustrophobic, that he has not only been unaware of his own degeneration, but he has missed the newspaper account of Stillman's suicide over two months ago.

Returning to his apartment, Quinn finds that he cannot reassume his abandoned life; his place has been rented out, and his belongings are gone. He makes his way to the Stillmans' vacated home and burrows in. When he awakens to find food left for him, he does not ponder it, as though he has been cured of investigative impulses. He writes, and as his light, pages, and energies dwindle, "he wondered if the case was really over or if he was not somehow still working on it. He wondered what the map would look like of all the steps he had taken in his life and what word it would spell" (198).

City of Glass concludes with its narrator reappearing to relate how he and Auster, who felt guilty about not having been more solicitous toward Quinn, sought him out at the Stillman apartment, finding nothing more than the red notebook that would become the purported basis of this novel. The fate of Quinn himself, in keeping with the novel's other impasses, remains inconclusive, and we are left with a flurry of narrative disclaimers about the omitted, the inaccurate, and the indecipherable. *City of Glass* stands as the dubious consolation for readers without recourse to the truth.

Ghosts is a chilly, spartan version of the stakeout in the first volume of the trilogy. Its opening is deliberately formulaic, so as to underscore the metafictional scrutiny that this plot structure will undergo in this brief novel:

> The place is New York, the time is the present, and neither one will ever change. Blue goes to his office every day and sits at his desk, waiting for something to

happen. For a long time nothing does, and then a man named White walks through the door, and that is how it begins. (7)

Both the compression of characters into color names—Blue, White, Black, Brown—and the minimalist staging of these chesspieces create the sense of a parable by Kafka or an anti-play by Beckett (especially *Ohio Impromptu,* in which the mirroring of watcher and watched is similar to the treatment of Auster's ghostly figures). Time and again the narrator comes out from behind the screen to expose the artifice of this literary exercise ("The address is unimportant. But let's say Brooklyn Heights, for the sake of argument") or to gauge its development while he is sketching it out:

> Little does Blue know, of course, that the case will go on for years. But the present is no less dark than the past, and its mystery is equal to anything the future might hold. Such is the way of the world: one step at a time, one word and then the next. (9)

Having established these conditions, which include dissolving the suspense that usually serves as the glue for this genre, the narrator places his characters. Blue is the detective who has been hired by White, whom he has never met, to watch Black and record his movements. Payment is sent weekly through the mail. Blue has put his own life on hold in order to complete the case, which comes down to his purgatorial vigil from a rented room across the street from Black, who spends most of his time writing. Blue's attempts at judgment are perpetually thwarted by the utter blankness of his subject, whose very name indicates a blank or a black hole, blunt as a period. Black has "dead eyes that seem to say there is nothing behind them and that no matter how hard Blue looks, he will never find a thing" (71). Watching such a man is like peering into an abyss, or worse, as was the lesson learned from the "mixed doubles" Quinn and Stillman in *City of Glass,* the voyeurism of the detective tends to boomerang into self-inspection.

This latter effect is a particularly fearful prospect for Blue, a man who prefers the composure that sticking to surfaces promises. His surveillance gives him time to ruminate about his fiancee, whom he has deserted in favor of this job, and about the nature of his profession. Blue had always been as confident as a nineteenth-century realist about the words he used in his reports, those "great windows that stand between him and the world," but now he has begun to distrust his procedures: "It's as though his words, instead of drawing out the facts and making them sit palpably in the world, have induced them to disappear" (24). José Ortega y Gasset predicts this "clouding over" of language in his metaphor of the window and the garden, according to which the modern work of art foregrounds the obstructive nature of the language it employs and despairs of unin-hibited contact between perceiver and world.[23] Surveillance must be imperfect, a naive dream for anyone except an omniscient narrator or a proprietary author who plots and confers every shred of accountability in the world he constructs. No less disturbing to Blue is the gnawing suspi-cion that as shadowy a figure as Black is, he is more amenable to "storifica-tion" than the would-be Mrs. Blue, with whom the thought of the future yields nothing but "silence, confusion, and emptiness" (23). At least temporarily, it is invigorating to think that Black may lead him into a reality in which anything can happen, and he grows to like him, or at least what he imagines of him.

However, Black's meaning is so radically unconfined that it leads to a repeated cycle of seduction and frustration, and intellectual stalemate. As confounding as not knowing what to think is not knowing what *not* to think—not being able to rule out possible explanations. On the other hand, an Answer would merely call attention to the author's handiwork, for the imposition of a preconceived, solitary cause—the innermost meta-fictional coil—would cancel speculation altogether.[24] Blue senses that the rules of inference have been repealed: his contemplations slide off the subject he is shadowing and onto fragile tangents (for example, the story of the man who finds his father encased in ice, which not only reminds Blue of his own father, a detective who had been killed, but also of the "thick" window through which he has been trying to examine Black). He cannot distinguish essentials from coincidences. What results is the stasis of a self-incriminated inquiry comparable to such European fictions of the absurd as Witold Gombrowicz's *Cosmos,* in which the insidious "demon of symmetry" turns every detail—like a crack in the ceiling—into a clue that reverts to the chaos at the slightest touch:

> It was a hard task. Even if something were concealed here to which the arrow on our bedroom ceiling pointed, what hope was there of identifying it in this chaos of weeds and refuse, which in quantity far exceeded anything that could be done on walls and ceilings? There was an oppressive profusion of possible links and clues. How many sentences can be composed with the twenty-six let-ters of the alphabet? How many meanings could be deduced from these hun-

dreds of weeds, clumps of earth, and other details? The wall and the boards of the wooden hut similarly offered innumerable possibilities. I had had enough. I stood up and looked at the house and garden. The big, artificial shapes, huge mastodons of the world of things, reestablished a sense of order, in which I rested.[25]

But the respite from confusion is fleeting. Similarly, when Blue sees that a man named Black was the publisher of his copy of *Walden* (a book in which isolation and rumination are redemptive!), he is "too honest" to succumb to the delusion that this fact, or any of the others he has gathered, are readable clues (33).

Blue's principal discovery is that he is a prisoner of the case he has undertaken. He encounters his one-time fiancee with another man, and she attacks him ferociously for his crime of omission against her and for his treachery in leaving her for Black. But what really troubles him is the suspicion "that he is also being watched, observed by another in the same way that he has been observing Black. If that is the case, then he has never been free" (56). The philosophical repercussions of this suspicion bring to mind Berkeley's claim that to be is to be perceived,[26] whereby Black is actually the beneficiary of Blue's attentions: "He needs my eyes looking at him. He needs me to prove he's alive" (75). Blue mimics the scribbling Black, whom he thinks may also be employed by White, who is "underwritten" by Auster.

The notion of identity as a system of hostage holding hostage also compares with Kafka's horrific visions of the writer's predicament:

> Perhaps there are other kinds of writing, this is the only one I know; at night, when fear prevents me from sleeping, this is the only one I know. The diabolical nature of this process seems to me to be perfectly obvious. It is the vanity and the hedonism, which flutter around and around either one's own or another's form in a ceaseless search for pleasure until in the end, by this constant repetition, a whole planetary system of vanity is created.[27]

Kafka's complaint that he "ought to be able to invent words capable of blowing the odor of corpses in a direction other than straight into mine and the reader's face"[28] aptly defines the self-defeating quality of Blue's writing, which instead of leading toward release from the case causes it to fester and to contaminate all other pursuits.

To avenge the theft of his chance at a normal life, Blue turns his attentions to the cryptic White. He waits for his unknown employer to appear at the post office box where Blue's reports are sent, until a masked man arrives to retrieve the latest mailing. He eludes Blue and sends a warning with his next payment not to persist in his disruptions, but Blue is galvanized by the impact he has had, and he determines to keep "chipping away at each conundrum until . . . the whole rotten business comes toppling to the ground" (55).

He advances this decision by accosting Black in a series of disguises (whose efficacy may well have been compromised by the possible collusion between Black and White). Black proves surprisingly expansive, sharing several anecdotes about classic American authors, but Blue is neither edified nor consoled by the company of these ghosts. (One of their discussions, on Hawthorne's "Wakefield," a tale about a man who unaccountably deserts his life only to spy upon it from nearby, particularly indicts Blue and may not be the casual subject Black pretends it is.) It seems clear that Black is as feverish as Blue about the obscure motives that preside over him; nevertheless, Blue cannot shake the belief that Black and White are conspiring against him, nor can he sort out true targets within this vortex of unavailing associations of colors, writers, and common presentiments.

When upon Blue's arrival under a new alias Black pretends that he himself is a detective, brazenly impinging upon Blue's already besieged identity, Blue is convinced that White pulls the strings. Perhaps, he considers, they are both characters authorized, or authored, by White. This would coincide with the ontological handbook for character employment and treatment offered by Flann O'Brien in *At Swim-Two-Birds*:

> a satisfactory novel should be a self-evident sham to which the reader could regulate at will the degree of his credulity. It was undemocratic to compel characters to be uniformly good or bad or poor or rich. Each should be allowed a private life, self-determination and a decent standard of living. This would make for self-respect, contentment and better service. It would be incorrect to say that it would lead to chaos.[29]

Unfortunately for Blue, he occupies a novel that rests "in the hands of an unscrupulous writer"[30] who disregards Affirmative Action and Equal Opportunity Employment for the sake of his dark, despotic script.

Blue breaks into Black's apartment—Black seems to accede to it, to expect it—and steals Black's writings: they are Blue's own pointless reports. "To enter Black, then, was the equivalent of entering himself, and once inside himself, he can no longer conceive of being anywhere else. But this is precisely where Black is, even though Blue does not know it" (88).

As in *City of Glass,* the "whodunnit" gives way to a "who-am-I," and the infuriated Blue violently attacks Black for the awful ruse that encloses them both. In the end, however, Auster does suspend sentencing, as it were, and frees the protagonist he has been abusing from the labyrinth of the novel: "In my secret dreams, I like to think of Blue booking passage on some ship and sailing to China. Let it be China, then, and we'll leave it at that" (96).

The final novel in the New York Trilogy proposes yet another variation on the *Doppelgänger* game. The unnamed narrator of *The Locked Room* has been summoned by the widow of his childhood friend, Fanshawe, to serve as his literary executor. This annunciation grants the narrator purpose and voice, and indeed, given the professional breakthrough that publication of Fanshawe's works affords him on the one hand, and his growing attraction to the bereaved Sophie on the other, Fanshawe's absence occasions his substantiality, not to mention his textual existence. He and Fanshawe are one another's twin ghosts, one lying in the shadow of the other's orbit, so that the narrator seizes this opportunity to write himself into Fanshawe's place.

Even as the narrator begins to thrive, as he proceeds to "ghost write" Fanshawe, he learns that any conviction about the man is premature. As a boy, Fanshawe had a kind of heroic stature that was largely predicated upon his inaccessibility to his peers: "You felt there was a secret core in him that could never be penetrated, a mysterious center of hiddenness. To imitate him was somehow to participate in that mystery, but it was also to understand that you could never really know him" (24). He remembers Fanshawe as someone whose private gravity was at once mesmerizing and daunting; his benign indifference to his companions—his solem inwardness—stopped them at the threshold of intimacy, and it continues to confound the narrator, who cannot integrate the irremediably discrete details of Fanshawe: "In the end, each life is no more than the sum of contingent facts, a chronicle of chance intersections, of flukes, of random events that divulge nothing but their own lack of purpose" (35).[31] In accepting the challenge to pursue Fanshawe, he hopes to redeem two reputations. However, the narrator employs that most dubious of instruments, language, which cannot get outside of itself to evaluate itself. As he writes his biography of Fanshawe, as clues, testimonies, and words converge upon his appointed task (he is encouraged by his agent to continue to tap this resource), he keeps smudging his object with his own fingerprints. It becomes increasingly difficult for him to see Fanshawe except in terms of himself: he seems to be the uncompromised version of the narrator, who has been until now little more than a hack writer of reviews; he is the haunting presence in whose footsteps the narrator walks as he assumes Fanshawe's position in the life of Sophie, supporting himself by publishing Fanshawe's manuscripts. Absent, Fanshawe still commands a presence in his writings more prodigious than the narrator, for whom this project is "a cause, a thing that justified me and made me feel important, and the more fully I disappeared into my ambitions for Fanshawe, the more sharply I came into focus for myself" (57). He is Fanshawe's second—his acolyte, confederate, and heir.

Auster's debt to Hawthorne is even more overt in this novel. *Fanshawe* (1828) was Hawthorne's apprenticeship Gothic romance about a remarkable but doomed scholar who disconnects from the world and decays in solitude, while one Edward Walcott, who accepts life's ordinary involvements, earns life's fruits—most notably, the hand of Ellen Langton, who becomes his by default. That Auster christens his heroine Sophie, thereby recalling the name of Hawthorne's own wife, plays further upon the autobiographical nature of Fanshawe's destructive allure for Hawthorne, whose tendency toward remoteness, both in his private life and as a recurrent theme in his writing, is well known. Intriguingly, too, Hawthorne and his wife labored together to keep the authorship of this less-than-accomplished first novel a secret, once again prefiguring, albeit with different aims, the narrator's conspiracy with *his* Sophie in *The Locked Room*.

The stakes of the game dramatically increase when Auster's narrator receives a letter from Fanshawe that reveals that he is not dead but merely in self-chosen exile from his life. Fanshawe sanctions and commends the narrator's industry, as though the narrator is the crucial accomplice in Fanshawe's disappearance. Like his eccentric precursors in *City of Glass* (Stillman) and *Ghosts* (Black), Fanshawe has upgraded his penchant for hiding places—graves and boxes figure prominently in the biographical details the narrator uncovers—into a relentless, ritualistic privacy so severe as to be indistinguishable from death itself. Commissioned to compose a biography about him, the narrator undertakes the role of forensic artist: he will "kill" Fanshawe in his pages, executing the man along with his papers and bringing official closure to the case in accordance with Fanshawe's directive.

Nevertheless, instead of enabling the narrator to prosper within the confines of the life he has appropriated from Fanshawe (Sophie is the principal reward for his countenancing Fanshawe's deception), promoting the death is like eliminating the parasite's host. Marriage and financial security have seemingly freed the narrator to explore his own writing projects, but he founders, as though his talents were now under exclusive copyright to Fanshawe; to risk a pun that hovers over the whole trilogy, he has already been "booked." And as his archeological assault on Fanshawe yields more ambiguous and alarming information (the sister's schizophrenia, the mother's displaced incest), he is confronted with the intransigence of his own processes and behavior:

> We imagine the real story inside the words, and to do this we substitute ourselves for the person in the story, pretending that we can understand him because we understand ourselves. This is a deception. We exist for ourselves, perhaps, and at times we even have a glimmer of who we are, but in the end we can never be sure, and as our lives go on, we become more and more opaque to ourselves, more and more aware of our own incoherence. No one can cross the boundary into another—for the simple reason that no one can gain access to himself. (80–81)

The threat of psychological disintegration from servitude to Fanshawe is greater than the threat posed by Fanshawe himself that he would kill the narrator should he try to locate him. As Humbert Humbert sought out the iniquitous Clare Quilty in *Lolita,* as Zoe Bickle took off with documentary zeal after Cabot Wright in *Cabot Wright Begins,*[32] so does our literary biographer become a private detective, plundering Fanshawe's letters, novels, and plays for clues to his underground lair. The deterrences to the narrator's operations are formidable. Not only does Fanshawe's fanatical adherence to his cult of impersonality, not to mention his death threat against the narrator should he pursue him, ward off critical inquiry, but the narrator suspects that he is really looting Fanshawe's jetsam for his own likeness. The search for Fanshawe spirals in upon the narrator; the hypothetical "locked room" that Fanshawe inhabits is the narrator's own head (147).

The narrator's search degenerates into a slow descent into depravity and dereliction. He sees himself as a necrophile pawing at a dead issue. He arbitrarily deems a stranger Fanshawe (he protests he is Peter Stillman!) and pesters him until he is rewarded with a beating. He surrenders to outrage and "the vertigo of pure chance" (155). He even confesses his responsibility for the entire New York Trilogy (a fact that we have been prepared for in part by the early cameo appearance of Quinn as the detective chosen by Sophie to locate her missing husband, as well as by the familiar alias employed by Fanshawe, Henry Dark).

The narrator recoils from his adventure and returns to the compensatory comforts of domesticity and silence. In the end, Fanshawe does contact him again. Although he refuses to emerge from behind his closed door, he leaves the narrator his red notebook, which he promises will clarify his machinations; he claims that he has already taken poison, so he need no longer fear any interference from the outside world. Still, there is nothing revelatory about the contents of the notebook, which essentially double back upon the past novels in Auster's trilogy. As the narrator admits, the notebook stands as a last monument to the inexpressibility of Fanshawe: "Each sentence erased the sentence before it, each paragraph made the next paragraph impossible" (178). Faltering with each step, with each entry he encounters, he destroys the notebook page by page as he reads it, and we and the narrator reach the end of *The Locked Room* simultaneously.

Because it uses humor and raucous invention to deflect the consequences of its demolition of generic conventions, parody can shape other options than the anxious circularities of Auster's trilogy. Thomas Berger's *Who Is Teddy Villanova?* takes a playfully nihilistic approach to the detective novel even as it dutifully rehearses its usual features.[33] But whereas Berger's elaborate style is at the other end of the spectrum from Auster's spartan chill, *Who Is Teddy Villanova?* strikes blows against the empire of empiricism similar to those delivered by the New York Trilogy; specifically, it detours the empirical quest into linguistic, epistemological, and (as the book's title promises) ontological concerns.

Cutting the compulsory figures of the detective routine is Russell Wren, a decadent version of his hard-boiled predecessors in the business of private investigation whose very name implies a furtive nature and unprepossessing capacities when contrasted with the sharp edges of Spade, Archer, and Company. Surely the most obvious aspect of Wren's departure from those models is his sheer prolixity. Opposing the clipped reserve of the tough guy is the persistent rustle of purple clauses through the consciousness of the ex-English teacher Wren, for whom language, not action, is clearly the chosen realm of prowess. Berger opposes the grim economy of Dashiell Hammett, Rex Stout, and Raymond Chandler by dissecting, embedding, and protracting the moment. In place of the taut, stoic minimum, Wren's verbal style is excessive, saturated with literary allusion and exotic vocabulary:

> "Of course," I said, subtly inserting the tip of the wedge with which I might eventually cause him to topple, "if your statement proves unusually complex, there might well be some advantage in repetition, using alternative terms and varying syntaxes, not only for the sake of sheer verbal charm, but also with an eye to the state of affairs in the English language, in which, as one authority asserts, the only exact synonyms are 'furze' and 'gorse.'" (10)

> Until this moment I had not quite been able to rise above a suspicion that the entire affair, behind the screen of painted gauze, was the elaborate japery by which a pampered parasite, and his enormous retainer, sought to allay quotidian ennui. (172)

Terminally second-rate, this ex-English teacher of shriveled means and dubious prospects, his gun kept behind his two-volume Plato and his ego behind his puffed-up erudition, makes words his weaponry. "Call me Russel Wren," he begins his case history, invoking the ploy of Melville's Ishmael to adopt a self; like Ishmael, Wren will commit an ambiguous world to story so that, while its enigmas may remain insoluble, it nonetheless will feature and justify its narrator.

Who Is Teddy Villanova? is a rowdy eulogy for the detective myth it profanes with slapstick, pun, and sexual perversity. Like Melville's protagonist, Wren is abducted into a quest he cannot fathom, so he parries, though feebly, the physical and psychological assaults of cops who may be thugs, government agents who may be bit actors, and eccentrics who may be drug dealers by adopting the persona of Bogart-turned-pedant. All the while, Wren realizes that "the only real maverick is the criminal, and like most people I am but the occasional breaker of minor ordinances" (31).

Wren cannot even manage his own secretary, the preposterously innocent-yet-alluring Peggy Tumulty, much less sort out a plot that does not develop so much as thicken. Each clue is clouded by the cliché it recalls or the literary associations it triggers. Wren's "detection is (mis)guided by fortuity (alliteration), self-deception (epithet), and formalism (imagery)."[34] (At one juncture, Wren is required by the bizarre Detective Zwingli to submit to a quiz on obscure literary quotations in order to establish his identity.) As Wren searches for Teddy Villanova, whose metamorphoses potentially include most of the novel's cast of characters, including Wren himself (at one point all of his I.D.'s and personal documents have been magically forged with Villanova's name), he is beaten senseless or stupefied with vaudevillian regularity, so that we witness a repeated cycle of accusation, bludgeoning, withdrawal, and sluggish recovery. Repeatedly routed, and re-routed, by the sleight-of-identity, Wren suspects that beneath the morass of counterfeits and impostures lies a conspiracy whose very intricacy implies profundity. But the vanity that impels him—not only can sense be made, but I can make it—cannot be sustained indefinitely, for Wren is incriminated by his utter inability to distinguish real insights from red herrings. Wren flinches at every lead, digs at every plant. Instead of piecing the plot together in time-honored detective fashion, Wren is "framed" (both victimized by manufactured evidence and trapped in a tale fabricated by other narrators). Even his usually upbraiding secretary (he is perpetually behind on her salary) is moved to an "eloquent instant" of concern:

> "I got to thinking: a strange and sinister series of events has been taking place, Russ, and you are somehow involved, without your own volition, like the hub of a wheel which is forced to turn around and around yet doesn't travel anywhere itself, even if the car reaches California." (101)

The only thing that is not shrouded in confusion is that Wren is the target of hostile intent; not only is he physically abused and buffeted by contradictory testimonies, he must resist implication in homicide, drug dealing, and pandering. Wren can intuit the personal threat behind each incident or disclosure, but he does not have the savvy to penetrate its purpose: "Though particularly cryptic, as had been everything I had yet heard in this case, like all else its general significance seemed not to my advantage" (160), he thinks, while the elephantine Bakewell and his self-possessed superior, Washburn, collude over his fate.

The narrative rushes into so many dead-end alleys (including a variation on *The Maltese Falcon* in the form of a search for the legendary pornographic sculpture of Leonardo da Vinci, the Sforza figurine) that Washburn's admonition that "to remove the sense of wonder is often tantamount to emasculation" (165) seems superfluous at best. Meanwhile, Teddy Villanova is like a virus contracted by nearly all of the characters at one point or another. Typically, this anti-epiphanic novel draws to a shrug by steeping the proceedings in the mundane: Teddy Villanova does not exist, but rather has served as the axis of a byzantine scheme by Wren's landlord, Sam Polidor (many doors: an apt name for a landlord and for a canny plotmaker with no center but infinite circumference) to scare his last recalcitrant tenant from his building so he can sell off the property. That Wren never received the original buy-out offer—it was intercepted by Peggy Tumulty, who took it upon herself to hold out for more money—underscores the triviality of it all. Wren's indictment of an inept police force applies to Berger's entire crew: "Like all contemporary art-forms, theirs is in its decadence, occupied solely with structure and not substance, mere ritualistic role-playing" (229). When the landlord's game is revealed, *Who Is Teddy Villanova?* expires of exasperation; a subsequent telephone call from someone who claims to be the real Teddy Villanova, a Bavarian filmmaker who wishes to discuss his script, does not interest Wren, who foregoes the investigation of a transcendent "layer" and settles for a sexual encounter with Peggy. " 'It's too late in the game for me to be gulled again,' said I. 'I no longer believe in archcriminals and poly-morphous perverts. Quixotism cannot long survive among the Panzas of Manhattan' " (244). Constant deferral followed by cheapened epiphany is Berger's cure for wonder.

If Doctorow's Daniel Isaacson and Abish's Ulrich Hargenau are trau-matized by the chaos of human history, Berger's Russel Wren suffers from the scandalization of his mythic function. We have discussed Frank Ker-mode's warning about how fictions that are not consciously held to be fictive threaten to degenerate into myths, but it is important to recognize that while the parodist nimbly avoids this pitfall, the parodied hero actually aspires to mythic pretensions whose goal is a stable vantage point amid the turbulence of "mankind in motion."[35] Berger's Joe Detweiler, the protagonist of *Killing Time,* has so formidable an appetite for stability that he commits multiple murders to assert control. "Out in the world, try as I would, I could not get a firm grasp on experience," he explains. Consequently, he posits absolute visions of Justice and Death against the flux:

> I was incessantly distracted by the spectacle of mankind in motion, noise, color, the flow of all the different kinds of energy. I really started choking Mrs. Starr so that I could gain a moment's peace in which to think. (360)

Detweiler's methodical, grisly escalation of attempts to kill time—he moves from sculpture to taxidermy to embalming to murder—are like desacralized versions of the Buddhist urge to be delivered from the karmic cycle, "the hope to be freed from the weight of 'dead Time,' of the Time that crushes and kills."[36] If Russel Wren's mythic foundation is the hard-boiled untangler of knotted plots, Joe Detweiler's is the artist whose works (novels, canvases, or corpses) are bulwarks against temporal decay, or indeed, the saint who hypostatizes time so as to overcome its "killing" effects. "Each man kills Time in his own way" (366), Detweiler confides, but he misspeaks when he claims he is after "a moment's peace in which to think" because he is really hoping to achieve release from the lethal momentum of moments altogether. Quentin Compson tore the hands off his father's watch as a symbolic prelude to his suicide in William Faulkner's *The Sound and the Fury;* Tarrou moved from detachment and capitulation to absurdity—standing in movie lines and not attending the show, or waiting in doctors' offices without having appointments—to humanistic commitment against the terrors of Albert Camus' *The Plague;* and Joe Detweiler confers the "ruthless authority" of the imagination, both through his invented method of metempsychosis (Realization) to recuperate History, and through his homocidal approach to freezing Time and reforming its exigencies.

Whereas *Who Is Teddy Villanova?* determines that action "in time" is vain and unrewarding, *Killing Time* shows that the cost of escape from the temporal flow of events into the artifice of eternity is equally self-defeating. *Killing Time* opens with stern warnings against positivist inclinations that parallel the No Trespassing sign that hangs over *Adventures of Huckleberry Finn:*

> Readers are earnestly advised not to identify the characters in the narrative which follows—criminals, policemen, madmen, citizens, or any combination thereof—with real human beings. A work of fiction is a construction of language and otherwise a lie.
> Some years ago a notice was posted at the entrance to Sala B of the Uffizi Gallery in Florence: "Please don't touch the pictures! It is dangerous for the works of art, it is punished by law, and finally it is useless." [v]

Like the readers of Mark Twain's novel, Russel Wren is told he will be shot if he tries to ferret out ulterior meaning from the adventures to follow. Similarly, the police psychiatrists and detectives in *Killing Time,* for whom "the essential thing was to seem omniscient" (19), discover that the recourses of law and psychology are feeble indeed when stood against Detweiler's repudiations of causality:

> But what you must accept is that between a question and an answer, and an answer and an explanation, Time intervenes. You must not assume that, standing on a platform in the same place while the train moves rapidly along, you can step on board at will. (332)

So too is the media fallout that follows his killings unavailing. The sensationalist interests of newspapermen and biographers who attach themselves to suspects and survivors in the case are by and large disappointed, depending as they do on verbal testimony: "'You can't ever expect to Realize an act in words: what you are talking about is talk'" (303), explains the anti-literate Detweiler. He dismisses curiosity as bankrupt and seeks to stop the progress of time on which reading epiphany at least hypothetically depends.

Alan Wilde depicts Thomas Berger's fiction as a systematic demystification of "the imperial ego: the self as a preexistent 'psychic entity' coercing a yielding world into a transparent text."[37] Berger mocks the probing "intentionality of consciousness" on the grounds "that human beings are immersed, embedded, in the world, inseparable from it and incapable of attaining some ideal, neutral, detached vantage point from which to take its measure" and "that because consciousness is situated, it is inevitably partial, limited and perspectival."[38] Accordingly, *Who Is Teddy Villanova?* exchanges hard-boiled causality for half-baked contrivance, and *Killing Time* simply abdicates the edifying pretense of art. The bookish Wren and Detweiler, who has given up reading as futile, arrive at the same state of exasperation in the face of the Indeterminate. Along with Auster's anti-detectives, they have been barred from the fraternity of competence and divination that Robert Coover's Inspector Pardew ridicules in *Gerald's Party,* another striptease of the genre. Parody is their vengeance for being blackballed.

The old apparatus of detection has depreciated into a nostalgic bluff. Its once-tenacious ideology has fallen into disrepute. As Leonard Michaels writes, "Real ideas strike like eagles. A man who loves premises and conclusions loves a whore."[39] Unfortunately, as we learned from William Spanos in Chapter One, neither instant revelations nor those disclosed by forensic science hold up very long under the naked bulb. Explanatory projects are self-referential poems, which, in Gilbert Sorrentino's words, "obfuscate the world's reality, the *fact* of its perfect inexplicable face":

> Art for art's sake is not at all a dictum to be held in fashionable contempt. It is, on the contrary, a perfectly just and eminently sane conception, allowing the poet to remove himself from the audience that looks to him for a product that he has no hope of creating.[40]

The structural consistency of traditional detective plots represents in part the compulsion to confer upon synthesis the dignity of ritual; protesting against "tidiness," on the other hand, is corrosive metafictional doubt. The work of art, be it a detective's conjuring with data or a Detweiler's opposition to Time's lethal regime, is "never any more than the pattern it terminates in."[41]

In *Moving Parts,* Steve Katz appropriates both the designs and the disclaimers of postmodern detection. In this four-stage fiction of provocations and obstructions, geographic and linguistic searches alike are exposed for their incapacity to probe beyond the scope of the codes that constitute them. Katz joins Auster and Berger in viewing human consciousness as being imprisoned by the conventions that host it: the strictures of a rational approach to phenomena—a tradition of at-homeness and presumed stability that is so insidiously a part of us that we seldom notice its emplacement. "Feeling the need to explain, we live increasingly in language restrictively employed, and become anaesthetized to the unique opportunities provided by experiential actuality."[42] Only when conceptual habits fail to answer their cues do we become aware of their existence, as well as of their provisionality and their inadequacy.

Moving Parts rescinds, amends, embellishes, or discredits the experiences it relates by persistently confessing the indistinguishability of all of the ingredients Katz stirs into the melting pot of narrative. Fantasy, autobiography, interpretation, documentary, and photography compete, combine, and mutate until suspicions riddle the text like bacteria. Every statement reveals itself as, at best, a cast at meaning it cannot deliver entirely, or even consistently (as Katz's title implies). Therefore, the author cannot authorize anything; instead, he sets the reader loose in the playground of potential significance and "spooky reverberations."[43] In other words, as Katz admits in an earlier novel, "One can speculate about the veracity of these contents and decide for him, but whatever the conclusion it is still a matter of mystery that they exist at all, and in a form that can please or amuse us."[44]

Moving Parts opens with "Female Skin," an account of Katz's surgical removal of the skin of one Wendy Appel, with which he proceeds to clothe himself. By making literal (within the surreal conditions of this section) such reliable bywords of intimate encounter as penetration, possession, and shared feeling; by reifying an extra-marital (if primarily intra-textual) obsession in the metaphor of a total kissing of skins, Katz strives for a breakthrough that conventional fictional modes cannot provide: "It was confusing, but if it had been accomplished according to some system, that system was brilliant, perfect, infinite in complexity, interminable."[45]

Nevertheless, the seams of narrative contrivance show through; the price of ingenuity is genuineness. After all, is "peeling" this enticing Appel more pun than insight? To allay our misgivings—he is usually forthcoming about sharing them himself—Katz buttresses his story with photographs of the main characters, testimonies and reactions to his work-in-progress, journal excerpts, and a photostated copy of Wendy Appel's release form allowing him to employ her in this story. References to Katz's other fictions are also included, and Ronald Sukenick, Katz's colleague, makes a guest appearance (apparently in repayment for Sukenick's having given Katz a similar opportunity in *Up*). Katz goes so far as to spell out in detail the questions and intentions that underly his fiction and that should accompany our reading like a Michelin guide. All of this foregrounding parodies conventional means of trying to earn for one's novel a measure of reliability: "It's important . . . in this demi-monde of costume facade & plastic to have something real to hold on to" ("Female Skin" 13). Things are inscrutable enough without the additional obscurances of concealed allusions, private jokes, or symbolic layering: "The problem is to know how to deal with all this experience. It's so bizarre. It's so banal. It's full of roaches. It's full of mushrooms. It loses so much in the telling. It's much better as a story" (7). Katz insists that his story is uncorrupted by method despite the disruptive effects of that contention. By stripping away artifice, he reasons, he is conspicuously trustworthy. The "telling," however, infects every shred of worldly evidence dropped into it. Rather than verifying the story, the photographs, documents, and other assorted appeals to veracity are compromised by the absurd context of "Female Skin."

Yet another constraint for Katz to reckon with is the consternation of his wife, Jingle, over her husband's spending so much time on the page with Wendy Appel, thereby accusing him of a uniquely creative form of infidelity. Indeed, excerpts from his journal trace the author's increasing desire to have this woman, be it sexually or textually.[46] Jingle's intuition is sound. Wendy is tantalizing. Her willing vulnerability, her openness to Katz's imagination, makes her an ideal subject. Moreover, she is keenly attuned to Katz's fiction: "Read to Wendy from SAW last night till my throat was empty. She had a special smart response to the work, clearly detecting my insecurity in it, or calling the self-negating way my work has of proceeding—insecurity. She sure is right from a certain point of view" (13). So Wendy and Katz easily get under one another's skins, in a comic escalation of Joyce's use of metempsychosis in *Ulysses* that makes the investigation of the continuity of human experience quite literal. The exhilaration of a fresh perspective threatens Katz's other relationships, as the author, decked out in this strange fiction, shows off his "Female Skin" to his other acquaintances.

Does entering his character provoke insights or just innovative delusions? At one point in "Female Skin," a multitude of geese descends upon New York City—we remember Hitchcock's *The Birds*, as well as Barthelme's "Porcupines at the University"—and the birds begin to respond to Katz's leadership. Is this marvelous event a result of his inhabiting Wendy's skin? Or is it an isolated phenomenon? Katz chooses not to investigate this issue—he is getting anxious about getting on with, and out of, "Female Skin." Instead, he offers his analysis of a friend's artwork:

> This new work of art by Charles Ross has the capacity to cause the slow dissolution of whoever views it by irresistibly absorbing the light that makes up the viewer's own real substance. It is enlightening to watch art-lovers disappear as they attempt to look at this unique new masterpiece (I call it that advisedly). Before they go some of them suddenly 'see the light,' realizing that all of reality is dependent on this energy, nothing else is as crucial. You can see them in that instant of spontaneous illumination, an impressive flash in the pan, and then they disappear. This new work of art is perfect, because it is inimitable. Anyone attempting to scrutinize it long enough to figure out how it's made, inevitably disappears. This is not a warning. This is a round of praise. (19–20).

Aloof, yet absorbing, art is celebrated for being a repository of ambiguity that seduces us into surrendering to its unfathomable priorities. The tentative, shadowy conditions under which narrative is written likewise tend to disqualify even the least ambitious illuminations. In another novel, *The Exaggerations of Peter Prince,* Katz interrupts the proceedings to disclose as much:

> The light here, you see, isn't just on all the time, but it's switching on and off at a rate of sixty times per second because those electrodes in that fluorescent tube are constantly alternating their charges with this alternating current, and the fluorescent light with that quick-die technique I just described goes on at that rate. I'm not calling the light vindictive, or even frivolous. The light does what it's doing and leaves the rest to me, but don't think that this book isn't influenced by the fact that sixty times each second it gets dark in here, making over the period of years it takes to write a book, no matter how small each instant, an appreciable amount of darkness. This condition of intermittent darkness explains then some of the empty avenues in this book, gaps like highway right-of-ways through the timber, like missing teeth, transitions that

are unreadable because you can't see them, all the more easily explained now under the heading of Stroboscopic Blind-Spots.[47]

The main characters of "Female Skin" eventually join at "the opening of Charles Ross' show of solar burns, exhibiting the signature of the sun" (26), which, like the "callipygraphy" of Coover's *Spanking the Maid*, simultaneously exalts and ridicules the readers' interpretive impulses. Assaulting the text, we end up surrendering to the self-sufficient, centripetal nature of the artwork, enveloped just as completely as Katz.

The first section of *Moving Parts* concludes with Katz's negotiation of an imaginative and legal release from Wendy Appel. Although he displays the signed contract (27), he cannot divest himself of her influence: "Will it ever be possible to find out, and then to express what it is really like inside the skin of Wendy Appel? It can't be all so goose. It can't be so metaphorical, so literary, so cool and militantly goose" (28). Nor does writing out the episode to bury it in a book called *Moving Parts* purge him of its claim upon his consciousness. True, Katz does not include Wendy in his next work despite her having been at the events that precipitate it, and she fails to cast him in the movie she makes despite her previous promise to do so. Still, "Female Skin" clings to him. And for that matter, we have been "goosed" a little ourselves, captivated by an outlandish fiction that fastens upon us like a foreign skin.

"Parcel of Wrists," the next section of *Moving Parts*, presents a bizarre premise that "Trip" is supposed to substantiate and extend. On the contrary, the venture into reality is the imagination's antidote. But what sort of prospects can we expect from a journey to a place called Irondale?[48]

When a package of forty-three human wrists arrives in the morning's mail, Katz assumes it must forbode a "strange detour" in his life; his daily routines are perforated by the word "wrist," which "kept firing in my mind like a sparkplug" ("Parcel of Wrists" 4). He fiddles with the wrists, pores over the package, turns them into the components of concrete poetry, and eventually buries them in forty-three flower pots. A peculiar number to send, he thinks. Perhaps some significance will sprout from them.

The return address for C. Routs (see routes?) sends him in search of Irondale, Tennessee, but no such place exists. Undeterred, he amends the summons and tries Iron Hill, which turns out to be an unprepossessing place except for the commune lying just outside of town. On the conditions that he relinquish his name in favor of one they bestow ("Seven") and that he work to earn room and board, he takes up residence in the commune, an environment already several times removed from the insight he is after. (He chooses work on the sawmill, but we are only momentarily stayed by the possible play on the title of Katz's novel *SAW*.)

Living, working, and loving among the other residents of the commune, Katz senses his involvement in a constant bartering between appropriation and surrender, alternately adding to and emptying out himself. As soon as he completes the repair work on the mill, he takes up his quest again, now with renewed vigor: "That there had been 43 wrists in the morning's mail, and that I was to take Route 43 to get to Iron City, seemed to me no mere coincidence. I was sure I was on the right track" (15). Nothing can be without purpose, he figures, if it yields consistent patterns and prolific circumstances for fiction.

In a later novel, *Wier and Pouce,* this same priority is demonstrated when a boy who has taken a baseball pitch in the eye wonders if he is really seeing "space people" shimmering before him in the bowels of the sewer system that serves as his secret thoroughfare:

> He wished someone was there to see it too, because was it really moving there, or was it inside his head? One eye was not enough to know. "Space people," he shouted, "I love you." It was going to be like this for him, he understood, one eye open, flattening out what was there, the other swollen shut from inside, rendering the "truth" into all its dimensions, never ruining a good story.[49]

Maintenance of the contours of the "good story" vies for precedence with any reductive truth. Consequently, Katz's fictional quests may be redefined as the interplay among competing distortions, and the chief criterion for pursuing a given "dimension" of truth is not its tenability so much as its inherent prospects for pleasure and intrigue. That these may entail the sacrifice, or at least the compromise, of inferential reliability is a problem that Katz handles with relative nonchalance—especially in contrast to, say, Auster's detectives; it bespeaks superior Negative Capability, as befits the uninhibited reactions to randomness for which the Surfictionists are notorious.

Katz travels next to Iron City, where he is frustrated in his anticipation of consonance with the mythical Irondale. "I don't know what to expect next. I don't expect anything. The day composes itself minute by minute" ("Parcel of Wrists" 18), he muses; still, the chief event here—a visit to a Cherokee burial ground—distresses him. The greedy rummaging of tourists for relics they hope to piece together into "something that might be valuable" (21) seems to disparage his own elaborate attempts to connect the wrists to a significant origin. What is more, his Iron City escorts desert him and his car is stolen. Has he been the victim of a practical joke? Have his perseverance and ingenuity steered him into the humiliation of a dead end?

The boon awaits him back home. Whereas defamiliarization had occurred in "Female Skin" thanks to an ultimate form of transvestism, it now comes from the planted wrists themselves, which have begun to exfoliate, rescuing the deteriorating story with unexpected growth. To be sure, Katz cannot return to conventional storytelling after this, as evidenced when his attempt to turn our attention (and his own desire) to his old love affair quickly sputters (24). Everything else seems impoverished and dull. The grisly tale of a friend's mugging makes little impression; lovemaking is suddenly perfunctory, even horrible. Devotion to the strange plants rules out "digressive" habits:

> It took almost all my money, but there was no way I could scrimp on this new responsibility. Was it a hobby? Was it an avocation? Was it my new path? The plants had begun to so appropriate my energy and integrate my time with their welfare that my decision had to be that this was now my life. I should have hated the idea, but I didn't. I knew that I would have to get a job, and keep it, no screwing around anymore if my plants were to survive. What a novel and exhausting cause has arisen to absorb me. What a fool I am. (27)

The plants bloom into a kind of dictatorship. Their surreal, bursting growth shunts Katz into a small corner of his apartment. While their colors are delightful and their fruits—human body parts—astonishing, Katz feels threatened by their odorlessness, which renders them aloof (a trait that has also flowered in his own personality, as though through some shared parthenogenesis). He brings his blinded friend an eye from one of the plants, but the gift terrifies him. He tries to convince his lover to wear sample prosthetic parts from the newly harvested crop, but she too is outraged. Katz feels that his conscientiousness has been flouted, but he realizes that there is no reclaiming the customary life prior to this adventure: "From now on life will be almost impossible for me, and there is no way I can help it" (33). Katz cannot accommodate any person or occupation that would diminish his fiction's progress.

"Parcel of Wrists" concludes when Katz runs into Susan Kentucky (another symbolic provocation? another route to see?), who has apparently been trailing *him*. They immediately "consummate" their relationship when she accepts the body parts he has displayed like a travelling salesman spreading his wares. In this way, "Parcel of Wrists" reverses and reciprocates "Female Skin," where it was Katz who applied a woman's features to his own. All the same, the discoveries of the symbiotic relationship between Katz and Susan Kentucky and of the mirroring between the first two parts of *Moving Parts* are insufficient to demystify the proceedings:

> I sometimes try to put my finger on the one problem that caused this life that I have, to all intents and purposes, lived, to take the peculiar turn it did at a certain point. I think it's that I never really trusted the United States Post Office. I didn't really believe in it. If I had I would have done what I should have done in the first place when I received my parcel of wrists in the morning mail. Without thinking about it I should have wrapped it up again and shipped it back to C. Routs in Irondale, Tennessee, where it came from. When I consider it from this vantage I realize that could have made all the difference. If I had done that my life might have worked itself out by an entirely other set of priorities. (36)

Katz provides a set of photographs of the author's wrists, but is he confessing his manipulation, still stirring the fantasy-reality stew, planting more seeds in our imaginations for the fun of seeing what comes up, or merely offering his good-natured surrender to it all? As the components of *Moving Parts* conspire more articulately, ambiguity does not fade but deepens.

After having recomposed himself, literally and anatomically, in "Female Skin" and "Parcel of Wrists," Katz ups the ante in the contest between his fiction and the surrounding world. The third episode, "Trip," proves that Katz is not ready to resolve *Moving Parts* into a stationary meaning. "Trip" begins another journey, but it also connotes an hallucinogenic experience, and we are still on guard against trusting potential motives or messages. On yet another level, it warns against the delusion that language can transcend itself to inspect itself:

> Language is the medium, and the limitation. . . . What can never be said, is what's being told. Lies can be used in the telling, 'truth', as well, if there is some; it might take smoke in the eyes to make perception possible. How's your rhinoceros? Tell the truth. What rhinoceros? How presumptuous, self-righteous to 'tell the truth all the time'. That's the result of eating too many soybeans, the ultimately deluding drug. It makes you think you can tell the truth. Go tell it to your rhinoceros. ("Trip" 74)

To slip these bonds, Katz proposes in "Trip" to test the integrity of his fiction by superimposing it upon a worldly counterpart: the real (that is to say, cartographically ratified) Iron City and a real commune, The Farm.

Immediately, we face the problem of sorting out the relative standings of Katz's textual proxies from one story to the next. Shaving off his beard to reveal yet another fresh skin (and preferring a clean-cut image for inconspicuous Southern travel), the author relinquishes "the condition of being Steve Katz to assume the guise of the personal pronoun 'he', the Protagonist. He heads for the gates of Greyhound, shedding the qualifications of Steve Katz like a moulting of adjectives," and, replicating the aforementioned sorcery of Ronald Sukenick/Roland Sycamore in *Out,* "He is whatever he can be now, the vivification of the protagonist of Parcel of Wrists" ("Trip" 10). Paradoxically, the author's textualized presence, if never absolute and entire, cannot be evacuated either, and like a series of kaleidoscopic lenses, stand-ins or voice-overs, refracts the story's surface.

Weighing scenes, characters, and theoretical pronouncements against extra-textual standards of reliability yields similar results: "If everything is invented, then legitimate and suggestive comparisons between kinds of invention become possible, collapsing the old dualities of fiction and reality into a single epistemology."[50] On the other hand, there is no rescuing the contents of the story for objective evaluation once they have entered the universal solvent of narrative. As a result, what can be known about Katz's trip is a function of, and becomes overshadowed by, what can be *said* about it (his "Trip"). And to the Protagonist's chagrin, seemingly little can be said about it responsibly:

> Iron City as it is on its small hill brushes through his life for a few moments like a coming attraction, a few curtains parted, situated in its own integrity, a ripeness of itself just where it is, no fiction after all, but a place in its place, tended by its people. He feels too shy to violate it. (30)

Katz cannot strip off the skins of adopted selves nor alter existing charters in the real world with impunity.

The struggle to authenticate "Parcel of Wrists" inevitably revises it. Imagination leavens experience; experience is always structured as fiction. "With what precision can you measure the initiation of no experience?" wonders the Protagonist in "Trip" (15). The question is moot: whatever he is mindful of makes the page; since he does not know precisely what the expedition is meant to accomplish, he cannot afford to omit anything, not even passages flagged for deletion. Using a self-evident fiction, "Parcel of Wrists," as the standard of anticipation for "Trip," he recognizes that everything he collects may be equally precious and irrelevant, beguiling and daunting. "Even if he did it right, he'd do it wrong. There was no way to do it wrong" ("Trip" 18).

Escaping the distracting hype and froth of Nashville's Opryland, the Protagonist sets forth to concretize his imagined settings, buoyed by an "abstract sense of familiarity" (43) and the creed "Above all, make sense" (28). The latter reins in his speculations and transforms the unpremeditated actor of "Parcel of Wrists" into the wilful editor of "Trip."[51] But the unexpected lesson of "Trip" is that the reality of Iron City, hopelessly prosaic yet "so tenderly itself," merits preservation from the assault of sense-making: "It seems wrong to violate this place with my fictional presence" (45). The Protagonist's procrustean agenda pales before the delicacy of established environment: "The place is so precise in its own equilibrium of lives, so perfect in its virginal decay, that I don't want to ripple the surface at all, or drop the weight of my fiction into the real time of this place, altering their time even if only slightly" (47). His entrance is an intrusion and a displacement; exploiting this setting, for whatever reason, does it an injustice. The Protagonist feels himself to be a walking disturbance, and like Kafka's Supplicant, one whose presence denies things their wholeness: "You see, I have only such a fugitive awareness of things around me that I always feel they were once real and are now fleeting away. I have a constant longing, my dear sir, to catch a glimpse of things as they may have been before they show themselves to me. I feel that then they were calm and beautiful."[52]

The Farm, like the town, does not so much fail to measure up to the imagined version as exceed it. Put another way, the two versions originate from separate, if parallel, imaginations: "One is an invented commune, the other is an invented commune; this commune is conceived in the mind, this commune is blown from the mind of Adam" ("Trip" 61). The interpenetration of mindscape and landscape ends up obliterating all semblance of story. "Trip" breaks down into a series of self-reproving comments on the futility of the project:

> As you intensify your focus on 'objective truth', events on the outskirts get dimmer, events that also bear on the whole picture, and when you try to annex those suburbs the focus downtown gets dull. It's a mess. You've got to move in the dark. Truth is everything included. (73–74)

Actually the extent to which I wasn't there was an amazing experience. This was the first trip I had ever taken completely alone; that is not even in the company of myself, unless I chose to intrude myself. On the other hand, this is all bullshit. I was totally there all the time, no way I could squirm out of my identity as much as I sent envoys of personal pronouns and protagonists. Identity is always one thing. Knowing it is all the others, and as soon as I force a separation, perceive a separation, I'm making fiction. Fiction is inevitable. (76)

His own witness, his own scourge, the author cannot long suspend so enormous a weight of disbelief. There can be no commune of knowing because "reality" unravels under scrutiny into "realities"—private, contingent, defying assimilation. (The photograph of the televised *60 Minutes* examination of the Farm is a blown bluff, for by now no medium can move us to belief.) The author, re-coiled into Katz once again, sings a "disintegrating song" (75): meaning crumbles in his grasp, and, frisked for further motivation, the story peters out.

"43," the fourth section of the book, shows how the eagerness to connect necessarily rouses suspicions about how much coincidence and arbitrariness lie at the heart of any symmetry. The teeming collection of 43's that enters the author's life automatically triggers the desire for design that has abided throughout *Moving Parts*. Apparently, Katz continues to subscribe to a faith that promises that the whole—a meaning he can endorse, a message behind the repetition of this number, or just a symbolic resonance that compels and sustains narrative drive—will be greater than the sum of its oddly moving, meticulously gathered parts. No one could be more industrious, or fanatical, about drawing 43's into the magnetic field of his attention: news items, the occult, lottery numbers, cash receipts, ages, temperatures, and the rest of the glitter of statistics are culled and docketed to substantiate Katz's passion. Enchanting as the infestation of 43's may be, Katz also finds it a bit disquieting. For instance, would *any* number reward such vigorous investigation? Is this fiction a stocked lake, a stacked deck, a pre-needled haystack? As the number mounts in our consciousness, 43, prime and indivisible, grows more unaccountable for all of this accounting.

Katz's method in "43" can be read as a direct response to the "Truth is everything included" pronouncement at the close of "Trip." It reminds us of Donald Barthelme's swallowing down of loose ends and detritus, which leads William Gass to comment:

Put end to end like words, my consciousness is a shitty run of category errors and non sequiturs. Putting end to end and next to next is Barthelme's method, and in Barthelme, blessed method is everything. . . . Much interest is also shown in 'stuffing,' the words which fill the spaces between other words, and have the quality at once of being heavy or sludgy, and of seeming infinite or endless.[53]

"43" manages to quell the reductionism that characterizes previous moments in the novel, whose effect, were it achieved, would have been to settle for less—to arrest the mobility of *Moving Parts*. Actually, we are as slow as Katz to contain the urge to formulate a thesis: we not only notice that there were 43 wrists in that parcel and that Route 43 ran through "Trip," but also that the digits "4" plus "3" add up to seven, which was the name bestowed upon Katz at the commune. Perhaps we do not interpret these connections as an affirmation of his writing the way Katz does, but we do appreciate the coherence and take comfort in the possibility that we have stumbled onto something profound.

Katz extols these talismanic findings for their simultaneous subtlety and brazenness. "I was impressed by the fact that prime numbers arrange themselves along the series of integers in a pattern that seems not to be random, but defies mathematical description" (3). A sense of precipitousness raises to the level of inspirational art the sheer convenience of having 43's at hand to plug into the text. "43" offers a pared-down universe in which the clutches of correlation dependably emerge; 43's are intricately, assuredly plotted like a zodiac consisting of a single sign. In fact, repetition does not diminish 43's fascination. It is a remarkably elastic "protagonist," infinitely nuanced—tragic when assigned to an obituary, romantic in a wedding announcement, magical when affiliated with alchemy. An "indelible tattoo on the skin of my experience" (21), it seems to keep vigil over Katz like a precise destiny.

In *Gerald's Party*, Coover's Inspector Pardew warned that "rigidified memory" is a crime against reality. Or, to repeat the common law of anti-epiphany from Chapter Two, codification libels experience. Katz undertakes the same issue in "43." To systematize to the extent that "systems are tools" is to carve out a place and a purpose from the vortex of existence; however, "as soon as you depend on the system itself for the answers, start looking *at* it rather than *through* it, there begins to form a cataract of dogma over your perception of things as they are" ("43" 22). We might well argue that "things as they are" remain safely locked away in hypothesis, or that post-Kantian man is so securely swaddled in his own consciousness that a pristine perception is unavailable anyway, seeing how even Katz himself avers that "our possession of the world is tenuous" (23). There is some basis, therefore, for his concern that the extreme version of faddism—astrology, the I Ching, or 43-ing—is fascism. Katz pleads for objectivity at the same time he reveals the obsolescence of the apparatus that would provide it. But reading Jung, Katz is consoled on this point because Jung seems perpetually on the verge of totalization without ever attaining it: "Because it's 'imperfect' Jung's work continues to be amenable to human diversity and the risk of experience" (32). "43," uncenterable and uncircumscribable, displays the same advantage. Arbitrariness and absolutism are equally unacceptable; surely, neither is conducive to art, so Katz's fiction oscillates between these poles.

Trying to finish "43" once and for all could put mystery to bed, just as Jung's practice threatens to shoo magic from myth. Instead, Katz stokes possibilities alive. 43 becomes a methodology, an active campaign, which, like the planchette on a Ouija board, now seems pushed, now alive and moving on its own. Not even a doctor's signed statement that 43 is innocuous (he misspells the word—is it 43's mischief at work?) affects the cancer of signification. The very effort to address the number ensures its consequentiality and keeps this fiction going.

The escalation of 43-gathering is one more means of goading the world into participating in *Moving Parts,* thereby reviving, or manufacturing, the chance of "an opening onto vistas of unbounded clarity, suggestions of eternity" (45). While the original impetus for taking these grafts from all these pedestrian sources—that is, the memory of a gracefully spiraling graph of prime numbers from an old *Scientific American*—turns out to be a mental forgery, Katz feels vindicated to some extent by the prominence of 43 as a crucial measurement in Charles Ross's "star tube" sculpture. The cosmos confirms him, and 43 is apotheosized . . . until further calculation disqualifies the measurement as a constant. Thus, "43" only fleetingly delivers on its project. Likewise, *Moving Parts* effects a compromise that frustrates revelation but keeps the artistic enterprise intact. In Katz's eternally ramifying fiction, we happen upon a mystery marked Urgent— and unreturnable as a parcel of wrists.

Literature's great reward, says Stanley Elkin in the course of a representative celebration of verbal energy, is its rich, associative weave: "Connection, invention, and all the enumerate links, synapses, and lovely nexuses of fiction."[54] In other words—as Elkin attests, there are always other words—we worship structure, and fiction, no matter how indecorous or downright subversive it gets, is inexhaustible in its capacity for producing it. But postmodern verbal structures are virtual only: the wedding of "if" to "then," of Tab A to Slot B, is under perpetual arbitration. The spoils of Imagination's turf war with Reality are never so certain as the retrofitting of sentences. Meanwhile, the key to the universe glinting in the garbage dump seems just as tarnished, and just as precious, as what is wasted.

Consequently, as conjunctions develop within the novel, as nodal patterns emerge through repetition, linkage, and incremental progress, we have been taught by recent fiction to suspect all gains of forgery. Frederick R. Karl encourages our doubts in a discussion of the contemporary meganovel, a form most notoriously practiced by Thomas Pynchon, William Gaddis, and Joseph McElroy, when he accuses it of being especially deceitful by virtue of the profusion of connections and overlaps it offers. Because the meganovel's very size, complexity, and strenuous delineation tend to elicit a world with greater conviction than do slimmer, more refined volumes, we are perhaps less acutely aware of the meganovel's exploitation of signification, seeing as the artistic techniques to which signification is indebted are more thoroughly subsumed by the swarm of context. Metafictional confessions of counterfeiting methods, writes Karl, lead to the conclusion that the only reliable insight is that textual machinations that engender insight must themselves be transcended: "Uncertainty of observation foreshadows the uncertainty of all systems; suggesting that antisystems, by analogy, may mirror survival."[55] The detective's delicate relational web is spun about a hollow.

Karl's reasoning leads to a dismaying set of alternatives: categorical fictions that subjugate consciousness, or the abyss of mere plausibility, whose vertiginous effect is powerfully described in Don DeLillo's *Libra*, in which the Kennedy assassination, "the seven seconds that broke the back of the American century," threatens to reduce any effort of analysis (including the writing of that novel, we suppose) to impertinence:

> Everything is here. Baptismal records, report cards, postcards, divorce petitions, canceled checks, daily timesheets, tax returns, property lists, postoperative x-rays, photos of knotted string, thousands of pages of testimony, of voices droning in hearing rooms in old courthouse buildings, an incredible haul of human utterance. It lies so flat on the page, hangs so still in the lazy air, lost to syntax and other arrangement, that it resembles a kind of mind-spatter, a poetry of lives muddied and dripping in language.[56]

What makes the quest so pessimistic is not the absence of clues but their ubiquity. Like Pynchon's Herbert Stencil in his sea of teeming V's, one does not cease to believe, he ceases to disbelieve. The atmosphere of these novels is always edgy, premonitory. All externals have been tabled or scaled to suit the search at hand. "Was there a cadence of the city audible only to the true citizen?" wonders McElroy's Jack Hind.[57] Mired in his obsession, though, he cannot decant the essential from the everyday.

Chronic forager or architect of the possible, the embattled questor is exhausted by the onslaught of "mind-spatter" he is finally powerless to dispute, settle, or even moderate, and thus, may shut down consciousness altogether. This eventuality is presumed by Donald Barthelme when he characterizes contemporary existence as "skiing along on the surface of brain damage, never to sink, because we don't understand the danger—."[58] And its novelistic manifestation might be termed "anti-quest" or "incurious quest," in which the reciprocity between mind and world and the relative embrace of initiation that are fundamental to the quest tradition are absent even though its framework of plot conventions still stands in formal protest against obsolescence in our post-agnostic era.

A devastating world waits in ambush for the hero in withdrawal. The anti-quest exchanges picaresque vitality for numb disregard. Flushed out of the tall grass he keeps to, the hero sacrifices goals of influencing or understanding the world and just tries to cope. Life's exigencies do not elicit his interest so much as his nostalgia for "that self-immersed indifference to the contingencies of the contingent world which he had chosen for himself as the only felicity and achieved so seldom."[59]

A touchstone for this plight of recession is the "cosmopsis" suffered by Jake Horner in John Barth's *The End of the Road*.[60] His hyperconscious awareness that no one choice is intrinsically superior to any other results in physical and psychic immobility; the cure is a program of Mythotherapy: the regular assignment of roles to the befuddled ego in order to facilitate choice and the rudiments of participation in the world. His shadowy Doctor enforces the worship of hard facts—read the almanac, travel in straight lines to scheduled locations, teach prescriptive grammar—and sanitized encounters with simple, strictly defined alternatives. Even artificial choosing (according to qualifications of Sinistrality, Antecedence, and Alphabetical Priority) is preferred to the paralysis of indecisiveness. That Jake's "narrative masks" prove insufficient to contend with worldly complexities is by no means startling. Moreover, the strategies of coping that Jake adopts are just elaborate versions of the general plague of arbitrariness. Stalwart detectives could not coax reliable insights out of their fraying experiences, so reluctant questors denied their instincts can hardly be expected to improve on their performances. Following suit, James Purdy's *Malcolm,* Jerzy Kosinski's *Being There,* and Rudolph Wurlitzer's *Flats* hollow out affirmation by discrediting the very motivations that propel the quest.

"All things swim and glitter. Our life is not so much threatened as our perception. Ghostlike we glide through nature," writes Emerson in "Experience," promising as he goes on that although they may intimidate at first, initiations reward those privileged to have them: diligence will muscle us beyond "this evanescence and lubricity of all objects" to earn us "the transformation of genius into practical power."[61] How stunning a contradiction to this sublime resolve is Purdy's Malcolm, who must be bludgeoned into initiation. Whatever meaning his "short long life" may contain is in the hands of a dubious mentor, Mr. Cox, who recalls Barth's Doctor since he too directs the protagonist beyond his ability to comprehend his directions. In fact, the initial meeting between questor and quest-designer is quite similar to that described in Barth's novel. Malcolm is found nearly inert on a bench in what appears to be a calculated solitude; to be sure, he will return to these "golden" moments in his mind throughout his adventures, speaking of his bench as though it were a forsaken lover out of a pure, uncomplicated past.

Mr. Cox is a relentless prime mover who assigns the boy address after address and occasion after occasion to encourage Malcolm to "give himself up to things."[62] Malcolm's remarkable passivity makes him an easy victim of the lurid and sundry appetites of Estel Blanc, an undertaker; Kermit and Laureen Raphaelson, a midget artist and his insatiable wife; the wealthy, imperious Girard couple; Eloisa and Jerome Brace, and their entourage of musicians and sycophants; and finally, Melba, a popular singer, and her strange cult of "contemporaries." With each encounter, Malcolm's already tenuous sense of self-possession is further depleted by parasitic attentions, which are not paid to but exacted from his beautiful innocence. His succumbing to marriage with Melba is no exception to this rule, for in this novel, marriage is not the time-honored remuneration for the successful adventurer but just another exploitative maneuver.

In short, if Malcolm is "a cypher and a blank" (31) when the novel begins, his status really does not improve with experience. The houses he enters are tomblike, cluttered with stuffed animals and empty picture frames, while their inhabitants strike him as cloaked, protean (as evidenced by the shifting quality of Estel Blanc's skin color, Kermit's clothing, and Eloisa's age). At the undertaker's, Malcolm is overcome by incense and the mysterious song of Cora Naldi:

> And is it so that you were there?
> And is it so you were?
> And is it so that while you were
> Cherries were your ware?
> Pale cherries were your ware? (18)

Nothing matches the soothing fixity of the bench he was forced to desert. Mr. Cox chided Malcolm for his catatonia, but subsequent exposures inspire no alternatives:

> Everywhere in the house, no matter at what hour, one felt that it was afternoon, late afternoon breaking into twilight, with a coolness, too, like perpetual autumn, an autumn that will not pass into winter owing to some damage perhaps to the machinery of the cosmos. It will go on being autumn, go on being cool, but slowly, slowly everything will begin to fall piece by piece, the walls will slip down ever so little, the strange pictures will warp, the mythological animals will move their eyes slightly for the last time as they fade into indistinction, the strings of the bass will loosen and fall, the piano keys wrinkle and disappear into the wood of the instrument, and the beautiful alto sax shrivel into foil. (114)

The entropy of self and surroundings completes the faded spectrum of contemporary character referred to previously in this chapter. The ironic underside of the "fetishization of the inmost me," which has launched so many literary and personal searches for identity, is the "effective negation and diffraction of the self, a transgression of the identity principle,"[63] which leaves vacuous characters facing vacated premises. "You see," Malcolm complains, "my difficulty is I can hardly place any estimate on myself. I hardly feel I exist" (64), but his adventures do not provide him with substance—not even the confrontation with the man whom Malcolm seems to recognize as his father. Sentimental expectations are foiled as the man furiously denies Malcolm a reconciliation. That Malcolm is forever on the verge of dozing off comments both on his own hopelessness and on the depraved nature of a world in which the waking state seems rather pointless. When Malcolm dies, it is rumored that no corpse is buried in his coffin; since he was never wholly alive, death easily obliterates any trace of him.

"You aim at the primary truth: Why do you get up in the morning? Why don't you kill yourself? What sense is there in doing what you are doing? If you do not do this, you are still a being, but you are not a being *here* anymore; you are *being* there."[64] With this statement, Jerzy Kosinski incriminates his version of the "cosmoptic" cypher, who courts the usurpation of his own individuality by allowing himself to be governed entirely by chance—for which the protagonist of *Being There* is christened. Chance is "like a TV image, floated into the world, buoyed up by a force he did not see and could not name."[65]

Chance's state of arrest is even greater than Malcolm's or Jake Horner's. Whether his retardation necessitates his living in so restricted an environment (as the novel opens, his garden and his television exclusively demarcate his reality), or whether his hermetic stupor has resulted from these conditions is uncertain. In any case, the effect is less a matter of wilfull abstinence than of intrinsic uninitiatability:

> It was safe and secure in the garden, which was separated from the street by a high, red brick wall covered with ivy, and not even the sounds of the passing cars disturbed the peace. Chance ignored the streets. Though he had never stepped outside the house and its garden, he was not curious about life on the other side of the wall. (4)

Chance does not try to express, know, or evince himself; he does not seek a destiny. His quest, so to speak, is set in motion by accident: the death of the Old Man, his mysterious keeper, sets him adrift from the mansion into a world about which he could only have speculated, were he given to speculation, from the two-dimensional images of his television screen.

A walking blur, bereft of the documents and acquaintances that typically lend us social definition, Chance is struck by a limousine moments after his expulsion. Hence, the dying Mr. Rand supplants the Old Man as Chance's proprietor. What will make Chance appealing to Rand as a prospective successor to his estate, sexually beguiling to his wife, EE, and ultimately, available to meteoric advancement in the political arena is that he is an empty mirror: people see themselves reflected in his blank stare and bask in their own images. His pure complacency is seen as sober judgment; his homiletic pronouncements about the garden are interpreted as cunning metaphors for economic solutions. Diplomats admire him as a genius of understatement, and the President himself is so captivated by the mindless serenity of Chauncey Gardener (the renaming a consequence of mishearing "Chance, the gardener") that he quotes him on national television. Indeed, television, Chance's electronic pacifier while he was in the custody of the Old Man, continues to mediate between him and reality. Ironically, the man who is incapable of facing the world in any meaningful way is apotheosized into a larger-than-life savior through television "exposure": "Television reflected only people's surfaces; it also kept peeling their images from their bodies until they were sucked into the caverns of their viewers' eyes, forever beyond retrieval, to disappear" (68).

Wealth and celebrity, combined with popular indifference to complex truths, provide Chance with the same sort of insulation he enjoyed in the garden. In a sense, his prelapsarian ease never falters, so whereas Chauncey Gardiner may be ravaged by the masses, Chance, the gardener, retains his indomitable detachment (and is dealt a kinder fate than either Barth's or Purdy's heroes). At the end of *Being There,* his innocence has flushed away all of his experience: "Not a thought lifted itself from Chance's brain. Peace filled his chest" (148).

The plot structure that is so conducive to the hero's venturesomeness and relish for involvement is strained to breaking by characters who can no longer be stirred to curiosity. "Quest" seems hackneyed; with the ascent of Everest replaced (in Donald Barthelme's "The Glass Mountain") by clambering up a skyscraper with the aid of plumber's friends, it is hard to keep up the incentive, much less the grandeur of the enterprise. The postmodern knight, looking back down over "sidewalks . . . full of dogshit in brilliant colors" and a host of vulgar ordinaries (not to mention without benefit of Band-Aids to staunch the bleeding caused by an eagle's claws) proceeds "to disenchant a symbol" by steeping it in the quotidian:

> 97. I approached the symbol, with its layers of meaning, but when I touched it, it changed into only a beautiful princess.
> 98. I threw the princess headfirst down the mountain to my acquaintances.
> 99. Who could be relied upon to deal with her.
> 100. Nor are eagles plausible, not at all, not for a moment.[66]

Let princesses take their chances among the absurd rest of us.

Quest thins to extinction in the novels of Rudolph Wurlitzer. His characters are numbed itinerants or would-be recluses, all fatalities of postmodern skepticism. The odds and entities of *Flats* carry the names of cities, but they inhabit an unmappable environment; instead of granting them some sort of real-world priority, the place names parody the referential substance they command outside the text. Here they are odd nouns hooked to random gestures. Memphis, Omaha, Flagstaff, Halifax: all are gambits to emplace consciousness, pretensions of staking out space in the landscape and on the page. (I am *where* I am, as it were.) As temporary housings for the self—indeed, it appears that Memphis is the Ur-personality from which all others in this novel are abstracted—they enhance the narrative repertoire if only by varying the monotone of a single voice. The method is that described by Hamm in Beckett's *Endgame:* "Then babble, babble, words, like the solitary child who turns himself into children, two, three, so as to be together, and whisper together, in the dark."[67]

Beckett's shadow looms everywhere in *Flats,* from the stripped, post-holocaust, post-realist landscape, to the dilemma of the simultaneous urgency and incapacity of expression, to the declensions of the self. Like Beckett's Malone, Wurlitzer's Memphis distributes himself into stories that hold out the small guarantees of focus and momentum; to "make it to Cincinnati," for example, is at once a psychic and an artistic achievement.[68] Moreover, each new character that is introduced brings with him a fresh stock of attitudes and objects to inventory to help shape at least a circumstance, if not a destiny. Nevertheless, it must be admitted that Wurlitzer's "flat" characters are about as arresting as beer cans, bandages, toothpicks, and the rest of the debris strewn throughout *Flats.*

With its persistent interest in demarcations—angles and edges, gathering points and horizons, intersections and tangents—*Flats* is an exercise in spatial regulation. Self-definition is a matter of how space is imagined, occupied, embraced, or shunned.[69] Apart from these concerns, there is little to provoke the severely qualified articulations of character that Wurlitzer offers, and the novel's arbitrary rendezvous quickly succumbs to the emptiness. The anti-detectives of Auster, Berger, and Katz confronted a relentless raveling of options—what Pynchon referred to in *Gravity's Rainbow* as being "not a disentanglement from, but a progressive *knotting into*"[70]—that frustrated hierarchical logic by delegitimating it. The non-dimensional population of *Flats,* meanwhile, limp along without wonder. Omaha is "afraid of any concentrated act" (24); Halifax cannot muster any "semblance of intensity" (45); Flagstaff accuses Abilene of having "separated yourself from sequences" (65); Tacoma is praised for resisting any "whoring after affirmation" (116). The "uncontrolled stumble" of Wurlitzer's preceding novel, *Nog,*[71] spills out here into an undifferentiated verbal terrain where movement is as inadvertent as that of marbles clacking about on a table top. In their search for fixity and density, the helplessness of the characters to enact anything or to choose at all drains their tale of its feeble impetus and annihilates fictional means:

> We all want to move out, to imprint an image on another space. But there has been nothing established. There has been no information. Thank god. We are saved another adventure. (64)

Voices ooze in and out of first person until they sink into final torpor and silence—"the masochism of uncontrolled pauses" (88). *Flats* is like one of Yve Tanguy's self-destroying machine sculptures, falling victim to its own prohibitions against progress and engagement.

The American novel's heritage features a sublime faith that equates space with potential and freedom with reprieve from outside authority. The contemporary detective, however, feels confused, and often terrorized, by the saturation of clues and the frailty of the case he tries to build; and the contemporary questor is often less concerned with vigorously imposing himself on his environment than with reaching a last terminal—that is, if he can rouse himself to concern at all. The protagonists we have studied either freeze at the threshold of ravishment or, in the case of the incurious questors, withdraw from incentive:

> Oh Babys! Ah Babys! Whither now? Whither later? It's all the same. Among the celestial acts in the theatre of night, in the superdome of the firmament, where distance is a monotonous allegory of diminishment, a shifting of solar dust, a waltzing of matter to the tune of darkness, a grave passage of this and that, what does it mean that you are asleep, adrift in the spectral silt of the unknown? What has the relentless fury of particles to do with you? Pull your covers up to your chins. Sleep tight; another Baby day is on its way.[72]

As in *Flats,* where a "phantom immensity" (127) in the nameless distance refuses intention or approach, characters are bibliodegradable and beyond grief. Generic formulas, which typically serve as dynamic programs of constitution, identity, and destiny, cannot sufficiently locate them. Jaded by failed analysis or utterly diffused into language, they are dubious candidates for carrying off novelistic conventions. Repealing causality tightens the budget on heroic causes.

Chapter 5

Resistance, Opacity, and the Uncommunicative Text

> "The reader is not listening to an authoritative account of
> the world . . . but bumping into something that is *there*, like
> a rock or a refrigerator."
>
> —from "After Joyce," by Donald Barthelme

At the core of this study lies what now amounts to a tradition of insecurity about the communicative capacities of language. Gone is the conventional wisdom regarding our employment of language entrusted with defining us to ourselves and delivering ourselves reliably to others. ("Language most shews a man; Speak, that I may see thee," wrote Ben Jonson, confidently founding our best prospects for mutuality upon the clarity and precision of the words we inhabit.) By contrast, contemporary fiction dismantles the convention of wisdom, blowing the semantic cylinders that constitute and convey us. Knowledge comes down to a thick knit of sentences worn over the frail ego—an "I" like a dull dagger plunged repeatedly, desperately, into the rich pudding of one paragraph after another. Instead of bodying forth Self and Other into intimate contact, words are often violent projections whose recoil not only verifies isolation but threatens to cripple us further.[1] John Barth offers this ironic encapsulization of how every encounter holds the potential for ontological trauma and treachery: "We converse to convert, each the other, from an Other into an extension of ourself; and we converse conversely."[2]

The brazenly self-evident quality of this condition in current literature is manifested as responses to, and demonstrations of, the materiality of composition. Whether evidenced by the lavish confections of maximalists or by the lean abbreviations of minimalists, the hard, retardant nature of the medium masses at the surface of the story like an exoskeleton. Temporal outcomes are supplanted by spatial objects, resulting in fictions that strain at their referential tethers. It is as though writers were now working with a denser alphabet, one whose constructions compel a hypnotic glare upon details so intensely set on the page that they do not resolve.

Due to the heritage of relentless foregrounding of the artistic effort within the artistic product, which so consistently characterizes the major fictions of this century—think of the technical exploits of Joyce, the streaming consciousness of Faulkner, the peristaltic rhythms of Stein, and the self-conscious gamesmanship of contemporary postrealists—we have ceased taking for granted our intimacy with reality and one another, whatever the means—social or textual—of intercourse. And as the efficacy of language as a medium of communication is radically questioned, we find ourselves intrigued by the language object which obstructs our view, until we recognize, to reword Ben Jonson, that language most shows itself, for it has only itself to express.[3]

An appreciation of this re-evaluation of literary language requires that outmoded metaphors be identified and replaced. It is convenient, for example, to speak of the language of literary realism as it came to prominence in the nineteenth century in terms of transparency. Marshall Brown sums up the leading definitions of realism by noting the pride they share in the novel's ability to appropriate the world outside the novel: "They posit a continuity between literature and life and then invoke this suppositious continuity to window on the world."[4] Or, like semaphore flashes, words signify, then subside once their representational mission is accomplished.

But once the language used to conjure the world becomes more overtly poetic or literary, it calls attention to itself in the process of discharging its duties, and we are distracted by "the imperious being of words."[5] To apply Ortega's famous corrective image once again, we see not only the garden but the windowpane through which we peer. The formerly transparent medium is clouded; language leaves deposits in its wake, and we may note that the increasing translucency of language occasions its growth as a subject of study unto itself.[6] As for the myth of photographic or documentary realism as a means of recovering a pristine sense of what lies beyond the pale of narcissistic rhetoric, it is more or less reduced to a hypothetical point of departure which is left behind with the first word by all but the most anxious or naive. In short, we confront, in Susan Sontag's words, an impenetrable plenitude—the silent work of art:

Silence is a metaphor for a cleansed, non-interfering vision, appropriate to artworks that are unresponsive before being seen, unviolable in their essential integrity by human scrutiny. The spectator would approach art as he does a landscape. A landscape doesn't demand from the spectator his "understanding," his imputations of significance, his anxieties and sympathies; it demands, rather, his absence, it asks that he not add anything to *it*.[7]

The contention of recent fiction in this regard is that the orderly, straightforward transmission of meaning is no longer possible; in fact, it may no longer be a primary goal. Its sentences hyperextended or oddly collaged, its words burnished to self-evidence or abraded to expose the grain, fiction exchanges revelation through language for revelation of language. Words are the principal *dramatis personae* parading across the contemporary page. And when the sentence itself is the event which arrests us, when fiction asserts its own wrought, synthetic nature, and when representational requirements are disdained in the name of freeing the imagination for "purer" activities, we are forced to re-examine where the authentic experience of fiction lies. Ronald Sukenick uses the term "opaque" to describe that most demanding brand of novel which:

> exists in and for itself. It is opaque the way that abstract painting is opaque in that it cannot be explained as representing some other kind of experience. You cannot look through it to reality—it is the reality in question and if you don't see it you don't see anything at all. . . . Opacity implies that we should direct our attention to the surface of a work. . . . The truth of a page is on top of it, not underneath or over at the library.[8]

Sukenick is reacting to works by contemporaries who share his respect for the plasticity of the verbal medium.[9] Common to all of these authors is the redirection of readerly interest to compositional textures and overt skepticism regarding the signifying capacities (or indeed, the signifying intentions) of language. In Jerome Klinkowitz's terminology, the "self-apparency" of this brand of fiction, which is achieved by flagrantly eccentric reference, exotic metaphor or syntactical display, and all manner of blockage of the "flow" of the story, causes cataracts to form over the textual surface.[10] We read such novels as though descending a mountainside—slowly, feelingly, scrambling at times for stability. This is architectural prose around which the white page eddies, and we attribute to such prose all that "architecture" suggests: calculation, permanence, density, physical resistance, completeness unto itself. Accordingly, consciousness is not so much transmitted as it is erected, or deployed. Through words, narrative colonizes the space of the page. What Roland Barthes says of Robbe-Grillet's fiction is relevant to the contemporary emphasis on opacity: "Language here is not the rape of an abyss, but the rapture of a surface."[11] As words "harden" into self-sufficiency, the novel becomes a linguistic privacy that barely consults worldly models. It is "an arrangement in which the possibility of any parallel reality is usurped not by the veracity but the voracity of language."[12]

Of course, the blocking off of the world from the reader does not always lead to invigoration by the freedom to improvise enjoyed by the writer. Dispensing with the world from one perspective is mourning its un-availability from another. As Addie Bundren complains in *As I Lay Dying,* "Words don't ever fit even what they are trying to say at"; they are imposters, "just a shape to fill a lack."[13] So many modern characters are positively claustrophobic about their textual circumstances, sealed off as they are from the world both thematically (how many of this century's novels are set in prisons, asylums, and other enclosures?) and stylistically, in a prisonhouse of language. Familiarity with contemporary fiction cer-tifies the reader to engage in a common market of negative passwords—narcissism, solipsism, alienation—without fear of contradiction. It has been a telling shift of perspective from Jonson's "Speak, that I may see thee" to the lament of Eliot's Sweeney Agonistes, "I've gotta use words when I talk to you."[14] Digressions, crossed purposes, non sequiturs, and other conversational impasses are so pervasive that the point of dialogue seems to have dwindled into the simple fact of churning out words in company so as to achieve, if only temporarily, the illusion of freedom from one's essential solitude. (And you, *hypocrite lecteur,* insinuating yourself among imaginary relations, are likewise caught with your conventions down!) As the Self desperately tries to maintain his tenuous rule over verbal space, the other is reduced to a strut, an excuse for extemporization. We may recall Beckett's Celia, beloved of Murphy, who finds her every effort to establish abiding mutual relations with him confounded: "She felt, as she felt so often with Murphy, spattered with words that went dead as soon as they sounded; each word obliterated, before it had time to make sense, by the word that came next; so that in the end she did not know what had been said."[15] Words are too heavy from "negative accre-tions" to transport,[16] or are too brittle to remain intact. Either way, the moment of connection succumbs to the futility of statement. And as Martin Buber warns, "I" must encounter "Thou" through "the basic word" that "is a deed of my whole being, is my essential deed"; otherwise, "I" invoke nothing but objects ("thinghood"), the end of which is not reciprocity but fetishism:

> But they, having become uneager and inept for such living intercourse that opens up a world, are well informed; they have imprisoned the person in history; they have codified the fulfillment or the breach, it does not matter

> which; nor are they stingy with reverence and even adoration, adequately mixed with some psychology, as is only proper for modern man. O lonely countenance, starlike in the dark; O living finger upon an insensitive forehead; O steps whose echo is fading away![17]

Detached among detached objects, shut up in the treacherous surrogacy of words, Buber's modern man may not even notice the subtraction he has suffered.

Literature's systematic exposure of the inadequacy of words can be traced in part back to responses to the hollow sloganizing and bloated claims surrounding World War I. Novelists were suspicious of their own instruments, for words had been contaminated by foul usage:

> Few doubted that data had meaning which transcended the factual ways of representation; most had little faith in the ability of the mind and language to describe transcendence. Many writers did not deny the possibility of the existence of mind and spirit, but they refused to contemplate the meanings in words. Many authors and the characters they created believed that words might destroy meanings for a person. Abstract words were a shallow pose.[18]

In the 1920s, Paris witnessed the birth of what Kay Boyle called "a grandly experimental, furiously disrespectful school of writing."[19] Although Joyce was the leading exponent of this school, disruption and dislocation also found artistic equivalents in Ernest Hemingway's tight-lipped distrust of words like "love," "honor," and "truth" which had cried wolf all too often, and in William Faulkner's successive proofs of how the teeming interior life remains irremediably locked within the isolated consciousness, leaving our words to one another too poor and too few.

By 1929, the groundbreaking journal *transition* was highlighted by a proclamation composed by its founding editor, Eugene Jolas. "The Revolution of the Word" included the following dictates: "The imagination in search of a fabulous world is autonomous and intact"; "Narrative is not a mere anecdote, but the projection of a metamorphosis of reality"; and "The 'Litany of Words' is admitted as an independent unit."[20] Against the deterioration of the world's reigning ideologies, against the requirements of a stagnant literary tradition, here was posited the rejuvenating novelty of the novel. However, there was also implied in "The Revolution of the Word" the possibility that we, as human communicators, were the ones being revolted against. (The insurrection of language would not be limited to a single front.) As Jolas stated, or threatened, in the two closing points of his proclamation, "The writer expresses. He does not communicate," and "The plain reader be damned."[21] Thus, the artist salvages his stature within an uncertain verbal environment by christening a revised set of standards for the artistic project.

Since World War II, the debunking of the myth of transparent language has been led most notably by Samuel Beckett, for whom, as George Steiner explains, "the notion that we can express to our deaf selves, let alone communicate to any other human beings, blind, deaf, insensate as they are, a complete truth, fact, sensation—a fifth, tenth, millionth of such aforesaid truth, fact, or sensation—is arrogant folly."[22] Beckett's lesson is that silence is nature's verdict, and every dialogue, interchange, and appeal is a sham. Worse, like Watt, we suspect not only that our words cannot penetrate another consciousness, but that they do not even adhere to the things we wish to name: "For there we have to do with events that resisted all Watt's efforts to saddle them with meaning, and a formula, so that he could neither think of them, nor speak of them, but only suffer them."[23] And in novels which are self-evident about their textual nature, characters know themselves to be quite literally bodies of words which must rely on speech to keep themselves alive. If they are suspicious that the repetitions they rely upon, like ceremonial incantations, represent stagnations from a larger perspective, as they are sucked into the vortex of the language they produce, they also believe that to have nothing to say is to greet extinction. Here is the Self self-saturated, at once announced and barricaded by verbal display:

> For to end yet again skull alone in a dark place pent bowed on a board to begin. Long thus to begin till the place fades followed by the board long after. For to end yet again skull alone in the dark the void no neck no face just the box last used to gleam in the dark on and off used to glimmer a remain. Remains of the days of the light of day never light so faint as theirs so pale. Thus then the skull makes to glimmer again in lieu of going out. There in the end all at once or by degrees there dawns and magic lingers a leaden dawn. By degrees less dark till final grey or all at once as if switched on grey sand as far as eye can see beneath grey cloudless sky same grey. Skull last place of all black void within without till all at once or by degrees at last this leaden dawn checked no sooner dawned. Grey cloudless sky grey sand as far as eye can see long desert to begin. Sand pale as dust ah but dust indeed deep to engulf the haughtiest monuments which too it once was here and there.[24]

What an effort, what a leap of faith, the discharging of that word "haughtiest" represents! But if this is communication dropping to zero, there is compensation, too: the insistent texturing, the wonderful rhythms. If, as so many readers complain, Beckett is a writer of exhaustion, it is a lyrical defeat he goes down to. And after all, there is the narrative itself, a dependable firmness which causes us to dwell on its opaque presence.

Whether or not this is sufficient compensation for being confined by the very words that tradition alleges will lead the Self out of confinement is another question. Despite the momentary illusion of prowess that commanding language may afford, the Self is often injured rather than vindicated by its narrative. In the estimation of the acclaimed language theorist Mikhail Bakhtin, to whom our environment is a "logosphere" and to whom experience is utterly dependent upon social grounding in order to enter consciousness, being and interaction are identical: "I am conscious of myself and become myself only while revealing myself for another, through another, and with the help of another. . . . Separation, dissociation, and enclosure within the self [serve] as the main reason for the loss of one's self."[25] Although this is a profound warning, the temptation to "amputate" the Self from the Other is perhaps increased by the rigors of living in a modern environment. The Self's reflex is to guard against exposure. Marshall McLuhan suggests a technological explanation for our reluctance to open ourselves to our environment, saying that social experience has grown too violent and superstimulated for us to endure; faced with the pressure of an overflow of external irritants (and other people are included among these), we numb our central nervous system against the tide. In this way, numbness, not openness, is our principal survival strategy. It is no wonder that Narcissus is consistently chosen as a symbolic father of contemporary man. McLuhan's analysis of Narcissus is most applicable to the fictional characters we have been discussing: "He had adapted to his extension of himself and become a closed system."[26] Forays into the world and encounters with one another are artificial precisely because the Self does not honestly contact anything outside its own rarefied atmosphere.

A stylistic equivalent of character as a closed system is the intensely self-referential novel. The text that mirrors itself seals itself in reduplication. In his *Long Talking Bad Conditions Blues,* Ronald Sukenick returns the blame for fiction's failure to recover the world to the world. The "blockage of articulation" is "due to accelerated shatter."[27] Art does not scorn sense, but is denied it. Narration confronts the precedent world:

> and the orderly harmony of the whole conception its beautiful artifice in his
> mind made manifest many marvelous meditations on measure as a mirror

managing doubling for those who found doubling troubling he had a theory that anything could be used to measure anything else as long as one thing was a conception and the other something to be conceived the mirror effect of one thing on the other making something of a nothing that would otherwise have slid into the oblivion of the unconceived not that this nonsense made sense of anything just that the notation of its happening made him happier a sensation highly welcome in a set of synapses stretched thin to snapping and so he strolled about Oldtown heavily involved in notation of its nonsense making use of many measures according to his theory for example a mackerel to measure a monastery a labyrinth to measure an ant a feather to measure a feeling a baseball team to measure a city.[28]

Opaque language does not seek to enter, nor does it contend with mysteries; the opaque novel is itself the completed quest, which looms mysterious before us. Recent authors strike out confidently, and often with a greater sense of playfulness, along trails blazed by Stein, Faulkner, Joyce, and Beckett. Raymond Federman connects the scouring out of psychological discussion by postmodern writers of "objectified surfaces" to a fundamental distrust of deeper levels of meaning: "there is a deliberate attempt to have the metaphors miss their targets and to desymbolize the fiction."[29] Language accumulates not to drive the narrative forward but to fortify itself against signifying aims. Gilbert Sorrentino claims that "the detail forms a kind of 'bump' on the narrative surface. . . . If there is no narrative apparent, the details *become* the narrative" and thwart the " 'lateral sliding' of metaphorizing."[30] Fiction that accedes to these principles does not work toward revelation, since it cannot know or illuminate any object outside itself with any assurance. On the contrary, it presumes that fiction is intransitive, one more "motionless object" for us to pass through or move around.

Appropriately, many of the defining features of the contemporary novel demand that we borrow terminology from the plastic arts to handle them. Donald Barthelme's high-intensity instances of cultural detail, for example, typically inspire comparisons to collage, in which juxtaposition and superimposition of prose fragments crowd out sequential progress and the grammatical march of significance. Barthelme's *Snow White,* along with works like Renata Adler's *Speedboat* and Kurt Vonnegut's *Slaughterhouse-Five,* turn reading into a kind of island-hopping from small section to section of consciousness adrift in the white space of the book. The combinatory passions of Barthelme's "Bone Bubbles" demonstrate the author's respect for the chaos of the elements he regards; Barthelme abjures finalizing the possibilities inherent in his appropriations of the blank page. The jostling fragments invite our creative collaboration, encouraging us to perform our own associations within and among the fifteen segments of the story:

> bins black and green seventh eighth rehearsal pings a bit fussy at times fair scattering grand and exciting world of his fabrication topple out against surface irregularities fragilization of the gut constitutive misrecognitions of the ego most mature artist then in Regina loops of chain into a box several feet away Hiltons and Ritzes fault-tracing forty whacks active enthusiasm old cell is darker and they use the "Don't Know" category less often than younger people I am glad to be here and intent to do what I can to remain mangle stools tables bases and pedestals without my tree, which gives me rest hot pipe stacked up cellos spend the semi-private parts of their lives wailing.[31]

And on it goes into its permutations, each piece seemingly polished from the sorting like Molloy's humble, precious stones sucked smooth. This is writing as rehearsal for writing—epiphany in outline only, invulnerable to foreclosure. In stories like "Bone Bubbles" or "Sentence," a self-conscious serpent powered by its own disclaimers—"a disappointment, to be sure, but it reminds us that the sentence itself is a man-made object, not the one we wanted of course, but still a construction of man"[32]— Barthelme's "gut constitutive misrecognitions of the ego" level out text by obstructing hierarchical efforts and therefore artificially extending the reading process beyond its usual orientation toward interpretive ends. The artifactive impact of Barthelme's fiction, the massaging tide of language, has a blearing effect on us: it renders everything, from people, places, and actions to hybridized nouns and Cubist mutations, objects of equal status and interest. But let us not forget that Barthelme himself does not view this condition as a deprivation of aesthetic capacities: "Mixing bits of this and that from various areas of life to make something that did not exist before is an oddly hopeful endeavor," he insists. Barthelme's incorrigibility, his spirited syntactic riffing, is played out on ground cultivated by modernist authors and artists alike. "The sentence 'Electrolytic jelly exhibiting a capture ratio far in excess of standard is used to fix animals in place' made me very happy—perhaps in excess of its merit. . . . The flat, almost 'dead' tone paradoxically makes possible an almost-lyricism."[33] These are the same sturdy, if provisional, rewards of sculpture. And instead of meanings per se, we have a liberated field of meaning in the making.

Thus, we are interrupted in our worship of recontextualization of parts into wholes by tectonic formations and deformations that, whether engineered by a playful voice or an anguished one, respects discreteness. Complementing this sedimentary property of the verbal collage is contemporary fiction's penchant for set-pieces: freighted images poised and swollen like friezes for slow-motion inspection. To illustrate, we might briefly consider Ronald Sukenick's "What's Your Story" and John Hawkes's *Whistlejacket,* both of which make an awareness of the compatibility of verbal and plastic arts a central thematic and formal issue.

By insisting that "the work of art is a conscious tautology in which there is always an implicit (and sometimes explicit) reference to its own nature as artifact,"[34] Sukenick predisposes us to an ongoing awareness of the circumambient physicality of any fictional context. "What's Your Story" begins with a protracted description of two famous paintings, "The Sleeping Gypsy" and "Washington Crossing the Delaware," upon the study wall and over whose busy surfaces the narrator pans. Both the surreal circumstances of Rousseau's painting and the romantic traditionalism of Leutze's, once they are translated into verbal equivalents, are indistinguishable from the conventional renderings of setting—that is, until we either recognize Sukenick's imaginative burglary or, reading on, realize that everything his eye lights upon is immediately delivered into, and as, fiction. Memories, professional anxieties, sexual fantasies, views out the window, his wife's interruptions of the work-in-progress, and any impulse or emendation—"Natural repugnance for dead meat strike carrion"[35]—take up residence in the text. "What's Your Story" implies by its universal solvency that fiction is always and inevitably a mixed media production.

Unavoidable as well is our own penchant for storifying data, and this is the main focus of Sukenick's comedy. "One scene after another, disparate, opaque, absolutely concrete. Later, a fable, a gloss, begins to develop, abstractions appear" (154). What enables the writer to dispel his creative block is the awareness of the natural inclination of his audience to be seduced (or to habitually seduce themselves) into treating all phenomena as constituting interpretive environments: "End with illuminating formulation" (154). Imagination, whether that of the ravenous writer or that of the willing reader, abhors a vacuum, yet even the most beleaguered imagination has itself for occupation and company (hence, Beckett's ironic title *Imagination Dead Imagine*). In spite of Sukenick's often-quoted Mosaic Law from *98.6,* which instructs "how to deal with parts in the absence of wholes,"[36] there is no such threat as long as we perceive linguistically, troping and figuring endlessly. Art's *tromp l'oeil* potential is inexhaustible. Thus, when in the next story in the *The Death of the Novel* Sukenick acclaims and seeks to emulate the flight of birds—"Concrete. Innocent. Beautiful. No Meaning"[37]—he is promoting an unspeculative openness to experience that the very self-consciousness of the concept automatically negates. "Form," he attests in *Out,* "is where you look back and see your footprints in the sand."[38]

Since textuality homogenizes all depictions, "What's Your Story" is super-permeable. Real-world objects and persons can enter and interact with invented ones. The thin fictive shell of Sukenick's apartment admits the clichéd gangster Ruby Geranium and Police Sergeant GunCannon to consult with, cajole, and intimidate the writer from whom they emanate and who, aptly enough, goes by the name of Ron Sukenick. However aggressively Sukenick defies Geranium's wheedling and his offers of collusion, the fact is that they share a verbal basis of identity, born as they are in the same story. Similarly, the view outside the window is as depthless and weatherless as the paintings on the wall: "Pit in concentric pit lay sunken in the center of a huge concavity" (138). Even the narrator's emergence from the fiction he is preparing into thoughts of the "flat truth of today," as represented for him by the ancient writing desk he associates with "a lucidity, a balance, an obvious and unquestionable respectability," is forever held in context (139). Ruby Geranium exposes the whole setting for its flimsiness by gouging the walls with left jabs and flipping the massive desk with two fingers. "What's Your Story" demands accountability; as Ruby Geranium discusses his confidence game/protection racket with "Ronnie," he implicates all authorial procedures. Enter Sergeant Gun-Cannon, and Sukenick is accused of vice, conspiracy to defraud, avoiding the draft, and consorting with known criminals. The page he composes, then, is a hideout, a vortex, a mirrored surface, and a "potent concentration," which means that every one of those charges hits the mark.

John Hawkes's *Whistlejacket* intensifies the aesthetic comparison and dissension between written and visual arts. For its narrator, a fashion photographer and self-anointed "carnivorous watcher,"[39] the world presents an inexhaustible collocation of shapes, colors, and shadows that the artist must police into congruences. Photography so dominates Michael's approach to experience that he is prone to collapse every encounter into a disturbance, or provocation, of his field of vision. "It is my fortune or misfortune to see everyday sights as if holding the camera up to my eye when I am not giving photography a thought," he confides (57).

Accordingly, his confrontations are at once intimate and detached, concentrated and selective. All of Michael's reflections replicate his manipulations of his models, which conform to the photographer's priorities of stabilization, seduction, invasion, and possession. By transforming act into image, by "curling himself about his subject" (7), the artist completes his insidious embrace. He composes each scene into a resonant pattern, arranging brief notations into a tenuous conspiracy of coherence.

Such accomplishments come at the expense of temporal flow. There is a fixed, static feeling to *Whistlejacket,* and we may recall T. S. Eliot's concern in *Burnt Norton:* "If all time is eternally present/All time is unredeemable."[40] Fiction does not perform actions; at best, it commemorates them as a system of traces of lost momentum. The novel is punctuated throughout by considerations to this effect. Michael is always measuring the sacrifice of the "felt" life against the saving elegance of artistic form. The implication of writerly tactics is clear, as when the family buries the master of the Stapleton estate: "I thought the living scene might cease altogether and become the still picture from which we'd never escape and in which the casket would never find its way from the straps that supported it to the bottom of the waiting grave" (11). Michael is most provoked not by the emotional content of the event but by the odd way the "frame" would be "invaded" by portions of the minister's presence:

> If I had had my lights, my cameras, I would have multiplied the dappling of sun and leaves, deadened some leaves and made others more white and green, would have layered like crystal the light that fell on the burnished casket and on the purple velvet cloth that covered the center portion. I would have carried the color from the minister's stole to the thick cloth on the casket, portrayed the dead man in the grip of his priest, and the purple I would have caught forever would have brought to the surface the dark and bloody red that makes the religious color possible.
>
> But I had no camera. Thinking about cameras and photographs was inappropriate in these harsh circumstances. But for all that, I had my images and knew they could never fade. (13)

Meanwhile, like the photographer setting his lenses, the reader faces the predicament of "centering" his sense of things, getting acclimated, habituating himself to the textual landscape.

There is a plot to *Whistlejacket,* a promising intrigue of murder, subterfuge, and sexual escapade at the Van Fleets', where Michael has been summoned to design a pictorial memorial of the dead master.[41] But the novel displaces these interests to the periphery, in part because its self-absorbed narrator, fastidious and cold, his ambush like a mathematician's, has perfected a talent for operating at a remove. "It's only what the developed film shows me that I care about" (128)—these are the boundaries of Michael's devotion.

When the novel's center descends into the heart of the enormous portrait of Whistlejacket, the legendary champion whose form broods over the proceedings as General Gabler's portrait does over Henrik Ibsen's *Hedda Gabler,* and who serves as the spiritual foundation for the novel's foxhunting episodes, we meet its artist, George Stubbs, and learn that Michael's precursor also had that uncompromising aesthetic. Stubbs's principles required that the truth of the postures and parts he painted be confirmed by surgery. (As will Michael, Stubbs saw his incursions matched and perverted by the whispered secrets and sexual intimations of his patroness.) Ironically, art must deaden its subject in order to exalt it; as William Wordsworth put it, "We murder to dissect."[42] Whether a painter (Stubbs), a photographer (Michael), or a novelist (Hawkes), the artist suspends his helpless subject as surely as Stubbs's ingenious contraption of hooks, belts, and pulleys suspended a dead horse to await the knife and saw, or as a strangely related mechanism held Harold Van Fleet's casket to lower it into the grave. Stubbs's beloved, observing the artist's operations:

> could not say which was the more oppressive to her, the animal's panic, scrutiny of a lateral view of a horse with only a portion of its skin and subcutaneous fat removed, fear of disease, or the signs of carnage in which they spent their days. But the more their work continued through the third horse, the fourth, the more she marveled at her Stubbs, who drew exactly what he had dissected and whose only emotion in their outbuilding was the pleasure of concentration. (92–93)

As the subject decomposes, the artist composes, and in the end, the more precisely rendered subject is the one more distant from reality. Whistlejacket's success is that he is finally wholly an artifact, a product of consciousness and craft. Art supplants whatever it addresses; certainly Stubbs sees it as more precious than its subject, as seen when he prefers to save his painting of Whistlejacket instead of protecting the panicked stableboy from the suddenly rampaging horse.

This idea of removal from reality, whose literary counterpart is the debate over self- or anti-referential fiction, is also evidenced by the many palimpsests that are discovered in the novel. Not only is Michael a modernization (bastardization?) of the pioneering Stubbs, replicating his efforts and incentives with updated tools, but his task of recreating Harold Van Fleet in pictures—itself a version of Stubbs's anatomizations of the dead—is based on pre-existent pictures which he has been given to photograph. (Michael's hunt for his subject parallels the commemorative hunt held in the dead man's honor.) Van Fleet, an adulterer with philosophical pretensions and a taste for erotica, imitates and refines his aged father's satyric practices. Actually, the very book is a palimpsest of sorts, in that the tale of the Van Fleets is superimposed over that of the English animal painter of an earlier century.[43] So we have Hawkes's version of Sukenick's sunken "pit in concentric pit" drawing us down into silence and stasis.

Michael declares, "The photograph for which the artist strives has no story. Story is the anathema of the true photographer" (106). Ruthless in his impositions, Michael evaluates his achievements according to their opacity. The instruments, decisions, accidents, and other preparations that precede or occasion a finished work of art (like the fact that Stubbs's painting of a young girl originally included her mother, who sat beside her to mollify her and who was later painted out) remind us of the manufactured circumstances of Harold Van Fleet's death by his spooked horse, in which case the participants and their motives were "elided" from the official results of the inquest. In detailing the battling stallions painted on the bowl of Van Fleet's pipe, a kind of miniature Keatsian Grecian Urn, Michael looks forward to the artistic incursion that will eliminate them:

> I photographed them. Their final portraits—two—would have nothing to do with remembrance, unlike the pipe itself. One sight of the pipe and I smelled its rising smoke, saw the smoker. The camera, at least mine, did not admit the past. No matter what Alex expected, my photographs, especially those I took that week in Hal's room, would stand only for themselves. (131)

Appropriately, the widow's original photographs are scheduled for disposal as soon as Michael is through with them.

For all the similarities between the verbal and the visual arts, the significant differences actually show creations of language to be more completely divorced from their worldly referents (or better, worldly instigations) in the sense that their representational capacities are sparser. Michael is also an amateur etymologist, and he occasionally points out the failings of words: there is no singular for "buttocks," but photography can readily produce one; other arts cast forms and fancies that there are no nouns to name. It is an impasse which has a prestigious heritage:

> For all these reasons, then, any way you may look at it, you must needs conclude that the great Leviathan is that one creature in the world which must remain unpainted to the last. True, one portrait may hit the mark much nearer than another, but none can hit it with any very considerable degree of exactness. So there is no earthly way of finding out precisely what the whale really looks like.[44]

With characteristic finesse, the contemporary novelist redeems his work by shifting the focus from capturing reality, which is as elusive as Melville's Moby Dick or Hawkes's horses, to competing with its creations.

Certainly, assessments of the novel which rely upon verisimilitude are inappropriate to words that follow Beckett's famous appreciation of Joyce: "His writing is not *about something; it is that something itself.*"[45] As Barbara Herrnstein Smith explains, literary works of art have no "compliance-class," and their "essential fictiveness . . . is not to be discovered in the unreality of the characters, objects, and events alluded to, but in the unreality of the *alludings* themselves."[46] What we know from reading a fiction is that fiction. Keith Fort's short story "The Coal Shoveller," after opening with a conventional dose of description of his subject—the laborer he spies from his second-story window—quickly complains that even the leanest, most cautious adjectives percolate with connotations that escape authorial intentions. "By the time thinking has become words it has ceased to be self,"[47] he reasons, for words protect their own integrity. Tracking the story's potential tributaries to their respective disillusionments, the narrative vision is so dispersed that authentic postures wither and uniqueness is depleted. "I don't want to turn on the light because it would prevent me from seeing clearly out the window, but it is too dark for me to continue writing."[48] And so the story strangles on its deathbed confession.

The eligibility of questions regarding the fidelity of fictional components to the actual world is minimized by the elevation of constructivist activity to the reader's attention. The islands of consciousness in Kosinski's *Steps,* the typographic "playgiarism" of Federman's *Take It or Leave It,* the airless corridors of print in Beckett's *Unnamable* and Gass's *Tunnel,* and the "pneumatic phrases" of Wildman's *Nuclear Love* are all overtly built. So too are novels obviously predicated on schematic "pretexts": these include Walter Abish's notorious *Alphabetical Africa,* whose intake of initial letters proceeds incrementally chapter by chapter until the nov-el's center, at which point options are subtracted one at a time; Paul West's *Gala,* which is structurally indebted to the sixty-four three-groups of the messenger RNA chain; and George Crumb's *Black Angels,* whose en-abling devices include numerology and an analog computer.[49] To speak of these books is to speak in terms of stones, not windows. Supplanting the virtues of realistic rendering is the virtuosity of verbal manufacture. We do indeed feel like a captive audience inside such books, and we should not underestimate that well-worn phrase, for as their language solidifies, the books present themselves as absolute objects. We must adapt to their conflicting textures or be lost. *Willie Masters' Lonesome Wife* is a par-ticularly unsettling hostess, but a suitable representative nevertheless: "Now that I've got you alone down here, you bastard, don't think I'm letting you get away easily, no sir, not you brother; anyway, how do you think you're going to get out, down here where it's dark and oily like an alley, meaningless as Plato's cave."[50] To propose a sanctioned referential standing, much less conclusive explanatory rulership, in the "dark and oily" confines of fiction is merely nostalgic, and the raising of the issue itself contaminates the field of inquiry with self-reflexiveness.

We have spoken of opaque fictions in terms of contests and discomfi-tures. With communication steered into ever-darkening passages, we must do more than ask how to interpret these fictions; we must also consider how best to appreciate an art whose theoretical basis seems to define the reader as a trespasser. This is ultimately an individual task brought about by individual novels. The freighting of the page to retard the forward march of the germane may compel the reader to wonder when the book will get on with what conventionally matters, only to miss the "matter" before him. However, in a general way, it is worthwhile to begin by recognizing the incessant self-analysis of works which wear their devices openly as a kind of quality control effort on the part of a genre which has suffered indictments of dissipation and irrelevance during this generation. When art contents itself with reflecting the familiar, it will obviously communicate to a larger audience, since it will enable the audience to find its bearings quickly and automatically. But it is important in evaluating the opaque alternative to recognize that reflecting the world is a compromise of the impulse to create something new and genuine. Setting artistic processes in competition against natural ones is a refusal to assign art a secondary reality serviceable to a prior one.

In short, opaque fiction forces a drawing up of revised contracts between text and reader. As Ian Wallace writes, "The outlines of opaque literature . . . are blurred, out-of-focus, or else the circumspection of the symbol is so sharp that there is no other meaning than the shape and context of the symbol itself; its permutations through space implying concepts or ideas about the act of reading in its own right instead of as a function of understanding."[51] Troubling with the hems and seams of sentences, contorting the conventions of the arrangement and pulse of language to startle the reader with calisthenic challenges, fiction heralds its flight from the ulterior. Survival *as* a reader is never guaranteed under these conditions, but there are bound to be casualties in art's war against habit. When the language of plot is transformed into the plot of language, reading becomes a constant renegotiation of meaning. Approaching opaque fictions like visionary landscapes (or perhaps, to acknowledge the skeptical, like biohazards), we learn to develop and utilize new resources. It is, finally, a pleasant irony that art which severely qualifies, even defies, communication *charges us* to respond. But attached to that response like permanent scaffolding must be our refusal to be beguiled—call it a wilful suspension of belief—which is the necessary etiquette of experience that rejects as it beckons. Art survives the sense we steal from it.

Chapter 6

The End of Value?

> Art is the reinforcement of the capacity to endure disorienta-
> tion so that a real and significant problem may emerge. Art is
> the exposure to the tensions and problems of a false world so
> that man may endure exposing himself to the tensions and
> problems of the real world.
>
> —from *Man's Rage for Chaos,* by Morse Peckham

"Once upon a time" is a cliché; it is also a covenant. This reminder comes
courtesy of modern-day advocates of reform in higher education for
whom the reinstitution of a unified field theory of values is high on the
agenda. *Which* values is seldom the issue, perhaps because the character of
our longings is a given consensus: "value" connotes Arnoldian rigor, a
whiff of ivy, and standards fronted by Doric columns. Rather, the conten-
tions of self-appointed curators of value typically announce the need to
sustain the grandeur of the concept itself, whose erosion is variously
blamed on a misguided appeal to relevance (followed hard upon by an ex-
coriation of the Sixties), neglect of traditional purpose, or sheer laziness.

This is a seemingly uncomplicated brand of conservatism, one that
depicts the genuine business of educators as the equivalent of canning
preserves and affixing clear labels to them for easy recognition prior to
storage in the Core Curriculum. Hence, Ernest Boyer writes, in *College:
The Undergraduate Experience in America,* that "beyond diversity, the
college has an obligation to give students a sense of passage toward a more
coherent view of knowledge and a more integrated life."[1] Disregarding
for the moment the built-in mitigations implied by "a sense of passage
toward" and "a more coherent view," we recognize a tone of missionary
resolve common to the most publicized complaints about the state of
higher learning. Whatever the source of the damage—intellectual relativ
ism, political compromise, or sheer trendiness in devising academic programs—the result is described in terms of disinheritance. William J.
Bennett declares, "We should, instead, want all students to know a common culture rooted in civilization's lasting vision, its highest shared ideals
and aspirations, and its heritage." Every college and university should

operate according to a "unifying principle" that bespeaks a vision of the humanities as "a body of knowledge and a means of inquiry that convey serious truths, defensible judgments, and significant ideas."[2] In "our eagerness to assert the virtues of pluralism," we threaten "to sacrifice the principle that lent substance and continuity to the curriculum, namely that each college and university should recognize and accept its vital role as conveyor of the accumulated wisdom of our civilization."[3] Bennett's catchphrases—"landmarks of human understanding," "civilization's lasting vision," "serious truths"—as well as his emphasis on continuity and heritage, clearly reveal his presumption that coherence is not something to be created so much as restored. If we restore coherence to the humanities, we will restore ourselves to coherence. Speaking as Chairman of the National Endowment for the Humanities, Bennett takes the concept of humanities as an endowment as unquestionable and unproblematical.

So, too, does his successor, Lynne V. Cheney, in her report on the state of the humanities in America. While Cheney differs with Bennett on definitions of the problems and cures, her fundamental definition of the standardized and standardizing qualities of the humanities is similarly absolute and confident: it is the avenue of direct insight fostered by "images of human possibility" and directed toward "increasing awareness of what human excellence can mean."[4] She exhorts schools to initiate questions in their students' minds that will enable them to discover these attitudes for themselves:

> Do they take away from their undergraduate years a sense of the interconnection of ideas and events—a framework into which they can fit the learning of a lifetime? Do they encounter the humanities in ways that make their enduring human value apparent?
> The humanities are about more than politics, about more than social power. What gives them their abiding worth are truths that pass beyond time and circumstance; truths that, transcending accidents of class, race, and gender, speak to us all.[5]

Once again, American education is charged with prodigality. Sublimities that we once possessed have been recklessly cast aside. Nevertheless, our concern here is not with the embattled canon itself, nor with the legitimacy of this or that structural revision, but with the fundamentalist assumptions about truth and value that underlie these protestations. Books—that is, the correct books—are depicted as bristling like cut oranges with righteous guidance; their messages are to be plucked, polished, and transported across the ages. Phrases like "transcendent truths" and "enduring values" are invoked without any hint of irony or self-consciousness. In their respective denunciations of our intellectual malaise, *The Closing of the American Mind* and *Cultural Literacy*, Allan Bloom speaks of "the good" and E. D. Hirsch "the necessary" as antidotes whose labels no sane reader could possibly misinterpret.[6]

A pre-packaged, consensual absolute, whatever its usefulness for adorning the revisionist doctrines we have alluded to, obviously contrasts with the skeptical models enlisted in this study. Need it be mentioned that none of these fictions has ever been drafted into service of the New Curriculum by any of its proponents? The incompatability of the protestations of Bennett, Bloom, and Hirsch, on the one hand, and of the equally notorious novels that nonetheless infest today's academic landscape, on the other, is substantial enough to suggest that they are really posing disparate questions altogether: whereas the former are asking what we should know, the latter are asking what we can know. Thus, Richard M. Rorty reminds us that "growth is indeed the only end which democratic higher education can serve," but "the direction of growth is unpredictable": "the social function of American colleges is to help students see that the national narrative around which their socialization has centered is an open-ended one."[7] In keeping with this belief, may we not claim that the promotion of alternative ideologies is not only literature's role but its inescapable nature? Meanwhile, the grand designs of educational theorists may themselves be fictions masquerading as spiritual law. Uncertainty infiltrates all but the most naive, or the most dictatorial, aesthetics: "Imagination, intuition, dream, elegance, beauty, interest: these, rather than the word 'truth,' occur most often in the discourse of workers at the edge of knowledge."[8] And "the edge of knowledge" describes the whole domain; everywhere—including the belly of the canon—is periphery. As contemporary fiction brazenly confesses, we do not solve, we cope.

In *The Renewal of Literature,* Richard Poirier credits Emerson with founding a tradition in American letters less brittle and uncompromising than its Arnoldian counterpart:

> the human situation in language, as Emerson imagines it, is barely negotiable; it is precarious, limiting, tense, belabored. To admit that this situation exists is not an admission of weakness, however, but of some degree of confidence, strength, and freedom. Suspicious that any word or act constitutes a commitment and is therefore immediately conformist, Emerson tries to define "ac-

tion"—as he tries to define literature—as something prior to publication. Action is to be located in the movement toward but never *in* a result.[9]

The energy of speculation is never dissipated by the conventionalization of final answers. The Great Books concept must be predicated on the conflicts and difficulties inherent in the ideas they elicit rather than on their hallowed reputation as ethical bastions. To simply absorb a cultural inheritance is to stifle this positive "action" by burying it beneath accepted intellectual commitments. When they are viewed as a self-evident, closed system, the words we speak "fate" us to truths grown heavy and implacable with generations of reverence.[10]

The political and philosophical distinctions outlined above recall the division between the Modernist search for "the still point of the turning world"[11] and the Postmodernist suspension of textual resolution. Perpetual transition, however disconcerting to conservative polishers of the literary canon, is far more characteristic of the style and substance of contemporary American fiction than their dreams of coherence allow. This is not to suggest that the seminal novels of earlier eras were unambiguous, only that ambiguity had been treated more often than not as a prelude to a unifying interpretation, whereby the critic surmounted textual difficulties to subject the work of literature to his reading—thus, the frequent appearance in New Criticism of approving terms like "harmony," "normalizing," and "resolution" that proved the recognition of paradox and difficulty to be the beginning of the end of confusion.[12] By contrast, when the ambiguity of texts does not drop away in deference to our compulsion to close off, interpretive activity must redirect its bargaining strategies. As Timothy Bahti indicates, an assessment of literature that resists New Critical pressures requires an appreciation of how terminology contaminates or predicts evaluations:

> ambiguity is *found* in literature, and represents a "value," a "richness," while indeterminacy surfaces in interpretation, where it introduces "impossibility or unjustifiability" of choice and decision, rather than the discovery of some value. Ambiguity is positive, indeterminacy privative.[13]

More often than not, texts are deemed not only readable but worth reading by virtue of these predispositions.

Leaving aside for the moment the justifiability of the desires for resolution, we still see that a prescriptive approach to experience inevitably disqualifies the works we have been discussing by refuting their depictions of experience as counterproductive at best, inhumane at worst. Simply stated, contemporary fiction refuses to be instrumental; it resists accounting, encoding, and time-honored legislation of understanding.

Yes, association makes a lovely web, but what belief would we presume to hang from it? Look closely: it is held together by serendipity and prayer. Howard Nemerov says as much in his *Journal of the Fictive Life:* "Symbolism itself is a suspiciously randomized way of sweeping up the world together and making it compassable as a single thought," while association is "the eye of the hurricane"[14]—all its charges drawn up about a blank. So where does the contemporary writer's propensity for shrinking from epiphany leave ethical considerations? What saves anti-epiphanic fiction from mere triviality?

In *The Company We Keep: An Ethics of Fiction,* Wayne C. Booth cautions us against terminological polarization—openness versus closure, and by extension, valued and valueless. Indeed, just as he finds didactic literature intolerable, he calls absolute openness in literature impossible to achieve, for both the intrinsic "adhesions" of words and the compulsive digestion of human minds automatically prevent it.[15] In any case, a purely indeterminate book would be a blank book; needless to say, its pages would never be turned. Booth instead proclaims "limited determinacies" as the practical compromise: an ongoing interplay between closing off and opening up potentialities. By openness, then, we mean a rejection of authoritarian opinion within as well as about narrative. To speak of anti-epiphanic texts is to imply numerous, competing ends and to refuse single-minded exploitation, which is not to be confused with the elimination of judgment. Quite the contrary, we are encouraged to vigorously appraise the challenge before us.

What is frustrating for one reader may be dynamic for another. It would be bad faith here to enforce a manner of appreciation. Instead, this study is meant to contribute to a way of seeing. The question is not what merits consideration, but rather, what constitutes consideration. More than ever before, our narratives "insist that we accept the doubt in the nature of our being human, while inciting our insatiable desire for a book and a world filled with significance."[16] Indeed, because they do not wear their meanings on their jacket sleeves, contemporary novels, instead of being denigrated as capitulations to irresponsibility or stupefaction, may be identified as models of restraint. Call suspicion heightened awareness and incredulity the advent of critical thought, and we may find that the most incorrigible fictions of the age *do* educate us. We are not dusting fossils but engaging the ongoing evolution of the imagination and its odd, elusive, captivating forms. As we may infer from the following admission by astronomer Vera Rubin, this sort of discretion is in keeping with the analysis of the extra-literary as well: "We don't know at all what the dark stuff is. We don't know very well how much of it there might be. The more we observe, the more doubts are raised." But let us not be misled. She continues: "Doubt is helpful. It wouldn't be as much fun to do science if every time you got an answer that was the end of it. Perhaps the strongest thing you can do as an observer is to find something that shows you need to learn more."[17] Tolerating doubt—relying on the initiations it provides—actually enriches our pursuits in the midst of "the dark stuff."

Throughout this book, then, we have looked at literature that, instead of settling for the deliverance of weighty, time-honored affirmations, offers a sense of what kinds of affirmations are still possible in light of the subversions of old pieties like epiphanic resolution, historical objectivity, literary convention, and linguistic stability. To regard morality in literature as being a matter of policing texts for turpitude would be inhibiting indeed. The prospect of reading fiction so cramped by accepted definitions that all of its moves were made with pawns would hardly inspire us. So contemporary fiction's ethical concerns are two-fold: at the same time that they interrogate received wisdom, they exhibit a drive for renewal, celebrating our insatiability for, and the apparent inexhaustibility of, fresh metaphors. There is as much promise as there is exasperation in Steve Katz's dictum that fiction is inevitable.

In the closing pages of Don DeLillo's *White Noise,* the aftermath of a massive "airborne toxic event" includes the transformation of the sunsets. At the end of the day, families, vagrants, lovers, and the elderly all gather to watch the sky flush with "content, feeling, and exalted narrative life." From the vantage point of the highway overpass, they witness in amazement as "the bands of color reach so high, seem at times to separate into their constituent parts. There are turreted skies, light storms, softly falling streamers." Halted by a vision beyond interpretation—it may be holy, apocalyptic, or indifferent—they are at a loss as to how they are supposed to respond. "Some are scared by the sunsets, some determined to be elated, but most of us don't know how to feel, are ready to go either way." Clouds do not diminish the view; rain merely increases the varieties of play in the hues above them.

The spirit of these warm evenings is hard to describe. There is anticipation in the air but it is not the expectant midsummer hum of a shirtsleeve crowd, a sandlot game, with coherent precedents, a history of secure response. This waiting is introverted, uneven, almost backward and shy, tending toward silence. What else do we feel? Certainly there is awe, it is all awe, it transcends previous categories of awe, but we don't know whether we are watching in wonder or dread, we don't know what we are watching or what it means, we don't know whether it is permanent, a level of experience to which we will gradually adjust, into which our uncertainty will eventually be absorbed, or just some atmospheric weirdness, soon to pass. The collapsible chairs are yanked open, the old people sit. What is there to say? The sunsets linger and so do we. The sky is under a spell, powerful and storied.[18]

This is the way the world reciprocates the attentions of contemporary American fiction. Its configurations concede nothing and everything at once; its displays overwhelm "previous categories of awe"; its offerings are not solutions but stories. Writers and readers of fiction may be reluctant to consent to these conditions, but that we must in order to be available to the marvels of unprecedented skies is the initial and perhaps the sole reliable revelation in store for us.

Notes

CHAPTER ONE

1. Quoted in Alfred Kazin, *An American Procession: The Major American Writers from 1830 to 1930—The Crucial Century* (New York: Alfred A. Knopf, 1984), 63. Despite the applicability of this phrase to my study, I admit that, in general, Thoreau trusts language to be more hospitable to, and evocative of, natural facts. For elucidation of his and other nineteenth-century American writers' attitudes on the subject, see Philip F. Gura, "Language and Meaning: An American Tradition," *American Literature* 53 (1981): 1–21.

2. Almost without exception, general studies of contemporary literature choose to grapple with the issue of periodization. Representative discussions of the Modernism versus Postmodernism question include Malcolm Bradbury, "Modernisms/Postmodernisms," *Innovation/Renovation: New Perspectives on the Humanities,* ed. Ihab and Sally Hassan (Madison: University of Wisconsin Press, 1983) 311–27; C. Barry Chabot, "The Problem of the Postmodern," *New Literary History* 20 (1988): 1–20; and Charles Newman, "The Post-Modern Aura: The Act of Fiction in an Age of Inflation," *Salmagundi* 63–64 (1984): 3–199.

3. Raymond Federman, "Surfiction—Four Propositions in Form of an Introduction," *Surfiction: Fiction Now . . . and Tomorrow,* ed. Raymond Federman, 2nd ed. (Chicago: Swallow, 1981)

4. John Gardner, *On Moral Fiction* (New York: Basic, 1978) 82. Further page references to this book are noted parenthetically in the text. For a broad sampling of responses by contemporary authors to the charges Gardner levels against them, see "A Writers' Forum on Moral Fiction," *An Anthology: Moral Fiction,* ed. Joe David Bellamy (Canton, NY: Fiction International, 1980) 5–25.

5. John Aldridge, *The American Novel and the Way We Live Now* (New York: Oxford University Press, 1983) 157. Further page references to this book are noted parenthetically in the text.

6. Bruce Bawer, "Diminishing Fictions," *Diminishing Fictions: Essays on the Modern American Novel and Its Critics* (St. Paul, MN: Graywolf, 1988) 5.

7. Donald Barthelme, "The Balloon," *Sixty Stories* (New York: Dutton, 1982) 54. Further page references to this story are noted parenthetically in the text.

8. Italo Calvino, "The Distance of the Moon," *Cosmicomics,* trans. William Weaver (New York: Harcourt Brace Jovanovich, 1968) 3–16.

9. Sir Philip Sidney, "The Defense of Poesy," *Sir Philip Sidney's Defense of Poesy,* ed. Lewis Soens (Lincoln: University of Nebraska Press, 1970) 35, 9.

10. Wallace Stevens, "The Comedian as the Letter C," *Wallace Stevens: The Collected Poems* (New York: Random House, 1954) 45.

CHAPTER TWO

1. Robert Frost, "Design," *The Poetry of Robert Frost,* ed. Edward Connery Lathem (New York: Holt, Rinehart and Winston, 1969) 302. Line numbers of subsequent references to this poem are noted parenthetically in the text.

2. Quoted in Walter Abish, "The Fall of Summer," *Conjunctions* 7 (Summer 1984): 118.

3. John Barth, "The Literature of Exhaustion," *The American Novel Since World War II,* ed. Marcus Klein (New York: Fawcett, 1969) 270.

4. Morris Beja, *Epiphany in the Modern Novel* (Seattle: University of Washington Press, 1971) 18.

5. Wallace Stevens, "The Idea of Order at Key West," *The Collected Poems of Wallace Stevens* (New York: Knopf, 1954) 130.

6. James Joyce, *A Portrait of the Artist As a Young Man,* ed. Chester G. Anderson (New York: Viking, 1968) 166–67.

7. James Naremore, "Style As Meaning in *A Portrait of the Artist,*" *James Joyce Quarterly* 4 (Summer 1967): 335.

8. Joyce, *Portrait* 232–33.

9. Robert Onopa, "The End of Art As a Spiritual Project," *TriQuarterly* 26 (Winter 1973): 363.

10. Mas'ud Zavarzadeh, *The Mythopoeic Reality: The Postwar American Nonfiction Novel* (Urbana: University of Illinois Press, 1976) 3–49.

11. Alain Robbe-Grillet, "Nature, Humanism, Tragedy," *For a New Novel: Essays on Fiction,* trans. Richard Howard (New York: Grove, 1965) 53.

12. Robbe-Grillet 68.

13. Claude Richard, "Causality and Mimesis in Contemporary Fiction," *SubStance* 40 (1983): 91.

14. William H. Gass, Foreword, *The Franchiser,* by Stanley Elkin (Boston: David R. Godine, 1980) xiv.

15. Jorge Luis Borges, "The Garden of Forking Paths," *Labyrinths: Selected Stories and Other Writings,* ed. Donald A. Yates and James E. Irby (New York: New Directions, 1964) 26.

16. Quoted on the dustjacket of Robert Coover, *Pricksongs and Descants* (New York: Dutton, 1969). Subsequent page references from this volume are noted parenthetically within the text.

17. William V. Spanos, "The Detective and the Boundary: Some Notes on the Postmodern Literary Imagination," *Boundary 2* 2 (Fall 1972): 149–50.

18. Spanos 152. Coover's Inspector Pardew, in *Gerald's Party* (Interlaken, NY: Linden, 1986), admits the limits of divination for the postmodern detective:

> Nothing, however . . . is ever so straightforward as it seems on the face of it. We have facts, yes . . . and all this associative evidence we've so painstakingly collected—but facts in the end are little more than surface scramblings of a hidden truth whose vaporous configuration escapes us even as it draws us on, insisting upon itself, absorbing our attention, compelling revelation. (283)

19. Alan Friedman, *The Turn of the Novel* (New York: Oxford University Press, 1966) 20.

20. Robert Coover, "The Magic Poker," *Pricksongs and Descants* 30.

21. Joyce, *Portrait* 213.

22. D. A. Miller, *Narrative and Its Discontents: Problems of Closure in the Traditional Novel* (Princeton, NJ: Princeton University Press, 1981) ix.

23. Ronald Sukenick, "The Birds," *The Death of the Novel and Other Stories* (New York: Dial, 1969) 163.

24. Robert Coover, *Spanking the Maid* (New York: Grove, 1982) 49.

25. Samuel Beckett, *Endgame* (New York: Grove, 1958) 57.

26. Patrick O'Donnell, *Passionate Doubts: Designs of Interpretation in Contemporary American Fiction* (Iowa City: University of Iowa Press, 1986) xxxii.

27. Thomas Pynchon, *Gravity's Rainbow* (New York: Viking, 1973) 25.

28. Kenneth Gangemi, *OLT* (New York: Marion Boyars, 1984) 4. Subsequent page references are noted parenthetically in the text.

29. Alain Robbe-Grillet, "Nature, Humanism, Tragedy" 58–62.

30. Charles Caramello, *Silverless Mirrors: Book, Self & Postmodern American Fiction* (Tallahassee: University Presses of Florida, 1983) 10–11.

31. Henry James, quoted in Carl Darryl Malmgren, *Fictional Space in the Modernist and Postmodernist American Novel* (Lewisburg, PA: Bucknell University Press, 1985) 69.

32. William H. Gass, "And," *Habitations of the Word: Essays* (New York: Simon and Schuster, 1985) 178.

33. Martin Price, "The Irrelevant Detail and the Emergence of Form," *Aspects of Narrative: Selected Papers from the English Institute,* ed. J. Hillis Miller (New York: Columbia University Press, 1971) 78.

34. William H. Gass, "Representation and the War for Reality," *Habitations of the Word: Essays* (New York: Simon and Schuster, 1985) 100.

35. William Carlos Williams, "Prologue to Kora in Hell," *Selected Essays* (New York: New Directions, 1954) 16.

36. William Carlos Williams, "Spring and All," *Imaginations* (New York: New Directions, 1970) 150.

37. O'Donnell, *Passionate Doubts* 67.

38. Richard, "Causality" 85.

39. Quoted in Marcel Cornis-Pop, "Working Theories of New Fiction," *North American Review* 270 (September 1985): 68.

40. Gilbert Sorrentino, *Odd Number* (San Francisco: North Point, 1985) 58. Subsequent page references are noted parenthetically within the text.

41. John O'Brien, "Third Degree," *American Book Review* 8 (May–June 1986): 11.

42. Quoted in Gilbert Sorrentino, "Language—Lying and Treacherous," *New York Times Book Review* 25 May 1986: 23.

43. Michel Foucault, "The Discourse on Language," *The Archaeology of Knowledge,* trans. Rupert Swyer (New York: Pantheon, 1971) 229. Sorrentino flirts with this issue in *Mulligan Stew* (New York: Grove, 1979) by prefacing the novel with a group of reviews of the book that may be either authentic responses or fictional parodies.

44. Quoted in the Epigraph to Gilbert Sorrentino, *Imaginative Qualities of Actual Things* (New York: Pantheon, 1971).

45. Wallace Stevens, "Sunday Morning," *The Collected Poems of Wallace Stevens* (New York: Knopf, 1954) 68.

46. John Gardner, *Grendel* (New York: Random/Ballantine, 1975) 55. Kathryn Hume similarly employs this passage in *Fantasy and Mimesis: Responses to Reality in Western Literature* (New York: Methuen, 1984) 169–70.

47. T. S. Eliot, "*Ulysses,* Order, and Myth," *Selected Prose,* ed. Frank Kermode (New York: Harcourt, Brace, Jovanovich, 1975) 177.

48. Alfred North Whitehead, *Science and the Modern World* (New York: Macmillan, 1953) 92. In *Process and Reality* (New York: Macmillan, 1957), Whitehead examines the linguistic aspects of arbitrariness: because "no verbal statement is the adequate expression of a proposition," we rely on established usage alone for the "false air of adequate precision" our metaphysical systems afford (20).

49. Saul Bellow, *Mr. Sammler's Planet* (New York: Viking, 1970) 3–4.

50. Katherine Hayles, *The Cosmic Web: Scientific Models and Literary Strategies in the Twentieth Century* (Ithaca, NY: Cornell University Press, 1984) 10. For a related treatment of issues of moral behavior and philosophical inquiry, see Jerry H. Bryant in *The Open Decision: The Contemporary American Novel and Its Intellectual Background* (New York: Free Press, 1970). See especially Chapters 1–3, pp. 3–113.

51. Quoted in Ann Jefferson, "Structuralism and Post-Structuralism," *Modern Literary Theory: A Comparative Introduction,* ed. A. J. and David Roby (Totowa, NJ: Barnes & Noble, 1982) 88. Significant treatments of how postmodern fiction does not comment upon reality but rather performs co-extensively with other real events include Richard Poirier, *The Performing Self: Compositions and Decompositions in the Languages of Contemporary Life* (New York: Oxford University Press, 1971); Raymond Federman, ed., *Surfiction: Fiction Now . . . and Tomorrow* (Chicago: Swallow, 1975); Michel Benamou and Charles Caramello, eds., *Performance in Postmodern Culture* (Madison, WI: Coda, 1977); and Jerzy Kutnik, *The Novel as Performance: The Fiction of Ronald Sukenick and Raymond Federman* (Carbondale: Southern Illinois University Press, 1986).

52. Susan Sontag, "On Style," *Against Interpretation and Other Essays* (New York: Dell, 1966) 36.

53. Molly Hite, *Ideas of Order in the Novels of Thomas Pynchon* (Columbus: Ohio State University Press, 1983) 14.

54. Bryant, *The Open Decision* 8.

55. Pynchon, *Gravity's Rainbow* 355.

56. Ronald Sukenick, "Film Digression," *In Form: Digressions on the Act of Fiction* (Carbondale: Southern Illinois University Press, 1985) 85.

57. Alan Wilde, "'Strange Displacements of the Ordinary': Apple, Elkin, Barthelme, and the Problem of the Excluded Middle," *Boundary 2* 10 (1982): 179–80.

58. Kurt Vonnegut, Jr., *Cat's Cradle* (New York: Delacorte/Seymour Lawrence, 1963) 137.

CHAPTER THREE

1. Philip Roth, "Writing American Fiction," *The Novel Today: Contemporary Writers on Modern Fiction,* ed. Malcolm Bradbury (Glasgow: William Collins Sons, 1977) 32–36.

2. Mas'ud Zavarzadeh, *The Mythopoeic Reality: The Postwar American Nonfiction Novel* (Urbana: University of Illinois Press, 1976) 7.

3. Isaac Bashevis Singer, "Gimpel the Fool," *Contemporary American Fiction*, ed. George and Barbara Perkins (New York: Random, 1988) 35.

4. Marianna Torgovnick, *Closure in the Novel* (Princeton, NJ: Princeton University Press, 1981) 5.

5. T. S. Eliot, *Little Gidding, T. S. Eliot: The Complete Poems and Plays 1909–1950* (New York: Harcourt, Brace, Jovanovich, 1971) 144.

6. In *A Poetics of Postmodernism: History, Theory, Fiction* (New York: Routledge, 1988), Linda Hutcheon coins the term "historiographic metafiction" to categorize the pervasiveness of postmodern refutations of "the natural or common-sense methods of distinguishing between historical fact and fiction" through indictments of the truth claims of both realms of discourse (93). "History requires, then, an edgy capacity for sustaining the enigma of irony," writes Linda Orr in "The Revenge of Literature: The History of History," *New Literary History* 18 (1986): 15. For other helpful discussions of this phenomenon, see Ilse N. Bulhof, "Imagination and Interpretation in History," *Literature and History,* ed. Leonard Schulze and Walter Wetzels (Lanham, MD: University Press of America, 1983) 3–25; J. M. Hexter, *Doing History* (Bloomington: Indiana University Press, 1971); Roger G. Seamon, "Narrative Practice and the Theoretical Distinction between History and Fiction," *Genre* 16 (1983): 197–218; and Mark A. Weinstein, "The Creative Imagination in Fiction and History," *Genre* 9 (1976): 263–77. All agree that we must move discreetly through the aimed, purposive plots tht histories mount in objective disguise.

7. Hayden White, *Metahistory: The Historical Imagination in Nineteenth-Century Europe* (Baltimore: Johns Hopkins University Press, 1973) 30. J. Hillis Miller also offers a run-down of strategies of coherence shared by fictional and historical form:

> They include the notions of origin and end ("archeology" and "teleology"); of unity and totality or "totalization"; of underlying "reason" or "ground"; of selfhood, consciousness, or "human nature"; of the homogeneity, linearity, and continuity of time; of necessary progress; of "fate," "destiny," or "Providence"; of causality; of gradually emerging "meaning"; of representation and truth.

"Narrative and History," *ELH* 41 (1974): 459–60.

8. Hayden White, Introduction, *Tropics of Discourse: Essays in Cultural Criticism* (Baltimore: Johns Hopkins University Press, 1978) 5–6.

9. White, "Interpretation in History," *Tropics of Discourse* 60.

10. Louis O. Mink, "History and Fiction as Modes of Comprehension," *New Literary History* 1 (1970): 557–58.

11. Weinstein, "Creative Imagination" 265–66.

12. White, "Interpretation in History" 60.

13. White, "The Fictions of Factual Representation," *Tropics of Discourse* 125.

14. Raymond A. Mazurek, "Ideology and Form in the Postmodernist Historical Novel: *The Sot-Weed Factor* and *Gravity's Rainbow*," *Minnesota Review* 25 (1985): 70.

15. White, Introduction, *Tropics of Discourse* 1.

16. Frank Kermode, *The Sense of an Ending: Studies in the Theory of Fiction* (New York: Oxford University Press, 1967) 39. See also Christopher Butler, "Scepticism and Experimental Fiction," *Essays in Criticism* 36 (1986): 50.

17. Cushing Strout, "The Fortunes of Telling," *The Veracious Imagination: Essays on American History, Literature, and Biography* (Middletown, CT: Wesleyan University Press, 1981) 6–16.

18. Bruce Robbins, "Modernism in History, Modernism in Power," *Modernism Reconsidered,* Harvard English Studies 11, ed. Robert Kiely and John Hildebidle (Cambridge, MA: Harvard University Press, 1983) 229–30, 243.

19. Lionel Gossman, "History and Literature: Reproduction or Signification," *The Writing of History: Literary Form and Historical Understanding,* ed. Robert H. Canary and Henry Kozicki (Madison: University of Wisconsin Press, 1978) 29–33.

20. White, "The Fictions of Factual Representation" 134.

21. E. L. Doctorow, "False Documents," *E. L. Doctorow: Essays and Conversations,* ed. Richard Trenner (Princeton, NJ: Ontario Review Press, 1983) 24.

22. Doctorow, "False Documents" 17.

23. Richard Poirier, *The Performing Self: Compositions and Decompositions in the Languages of Contemporary Life* (New York: Oxford University Press, 1971) 87.

24. Quoted in Bulhof, "Imagination and Interpretation in History" 9.

25. E. L. Doctorow, *The Book of Daniel* (New York: Random House, 1971) 262. Further page references to this novel are noted parenthetically in the text.

26. Doctorow, "False Documents" 21–22.

27. Murray Edelman, "Political Language and Political Reality," *PS: Political Science and Politics* 18.1 (1985): 10.

28. Quoted in Robert Erwin, "The Great Language Panic," *Antioch Review* 45 (1987): 427.

29. Geoffrey Galt Harpham, "E. L. Doctorow and the Technology of Narrative," *PMLA* 100 (1985): 82, 83.

30. E. L. Doctorow, *Welcome to Hard Times* (New York: Simon and Schuster, 1960) 125, 169, 178.

31. Doctorow, *Welcome to Hard Times* 156.

32. Quoted in Paul Levine, "The Writer as Independent Witness," *E. L. Doctorow: Essays and Conversations* 60.

33. E. L. Doctorow, "The Foreign Legation," *Lives of the Poets* (New York: Random House, 1984) 57.

34. Dominick LaCapra, "Intellectual History and Defining the Present as 'Postmodern,'" *Innovation/Renovation: New Perspectives on the Humanities,* ed. Ihab and Sally Hassan (Madison: University of Wisconsin Press, 1983) 48–49.

35. E. L. Doctorow, *Ragtime* (New York: Random House, 1975) 23, 68.

36. E. L. Doctorow, *Big as Life* (New York: Simon and Schuster, 1966) 61.

37. Thomas Pynchon, *Gravity's Rainbow* (New York: Viking, 1973) 164.

38. Larry McCaffery, "A Spirit of Transgression," *E. L. Doctorow: Essays and Conversations* 44.

39. John Clayton, "Radical Jewish Humanism," *E. L. Doctorow: Essays and Conversations* 117.

40. Cushing Strout, "Hazards of the Border Country," *The Veracious Imagination* 166.

41. Doctorow, "False Documents" 23.

42. Strout, "Hazards of the Border Country" 173–77; Paul Levine, *E. L. Doctorow* (London: Methuen, 1985) 184–85.

43. Richard Martin, "Clio Bemused: The Uses of History in Contemporary American Fiction," *Sub-stance* 27 (1980): 14.

44. Quoted in Levine, "The Writer as Independent Witness" 69.

45. Quoted in McCaffery, "A Spirit of Transgression" 47.

46. Ronald Sukenick, *Out* (Chicago: Swallow, 1973) 19.

47. Walter Abish, *How German Is It* (New York: New Directions, 1980) 2. Further page references to this novel are noted parenthetically in the text.

48. Walter Abish, "The English Garden," *In the Future Perfect* (New York: New Directions, 1977) 1.

49. Abish, "The English Garden" 5.

50. Abish, "The English Garden" 17.

51. Quoted in Richard Martin, "Walter Abish's Fictions: Perfect Unfamiliarity, Familiar Imperfection," *Journal of American Studies* 17 (1983): 234.

52. Hannah Arendt, *The Origins of Totalitarianism*, New Edition (New York: Harcourt, Brace, 1966) 458.

53. See Paul Wopitka, "Walter Abish's *How German Is It:* Representing the Postmodern," *Contemporary Literature* 30 (1989): 512–13. When refuge from interpretation is sought as a goal in itself, every new or contrary sign, regardless of its substance or intent, is a lesion in the reassuring complexion of the familiar. Its very intervention has the effect of terrorist activity.

54. Butler, "Scepticism" 62.

55. Dieter Saalman, "Walter Abish's *How German Is It:* Language and the Crisis of Human Behavior," *Critique* 26 (1985): 117.

56. Frederick R. Karl, *American Fictions, 1940–1980: A Comprehensive History and Critical Evaluation* (New York: Harper & Row, 1983) 552.

57. George Steiner, "The Hollow Miracle," *Language and Silence: Essays on Language, Literature, and the Inhuman* (New York: Atheneum, 1967) 99.

58. Susan E. Lorsch, "Doctorow's *The Book of Daniel* and *Künstlerroman:* The Politics of Art," *Papers on Language and Literature* 18 (1982): 389–90.

59. Don DeLillo, *The Names* (New York: Random House, 1982) 145. Further page references to this novel are noted parenthetically in the text.

60. Thomas Pynchon, *V.* (Philadelphia: J. B. Lippincott, 1963) 155. The demands of *boustrophedon,* in which the writing proceeds horizontally then reverses direction so that the reader has to retrace his steps to absorb a text, complements Pynchon's image of the difficulties of limited perspective, as well as anticipates the way Axton must recapitulate and reinterpret the data of his experience to digest it effectively. See Robert K. Logan, *The Alphabet Effect: The Impact of the Phonetic Alphabet on the Development of Western Civilization* (New York: St. Martin's, 1986) 37–38.

61. Pynchon, *V.* 226.

62. Don DeLillo, *Ratner's Star* (New York: Random House, 1980) 22.

63. Hayden White, "The Historical Text as Literary Artifact," *Tropics of Discourse* 50, 43.

64. Louis O. Mink, "Narrative Form as a Cognitive Instrument," *Canary and Kozicki* 143.

65. Paula Bryant, "Discussing the Untellable: Don DeLillo's *The Names,*" *Critique* 29 (1987): 18.

66. Donald Barthelme, "Not-Knowing," *Voice-Lust: Eight Contemporary Fiction Writers on Style,* ed. Allen Wier and Don Hendrie, Jr. (Lincoln: University of Nebraska Press, 1985) 37.

67. Tom LeClair, *In the Loop: Don DeLillo and the Systems Novel* (Urbana: University of Illinois Press, 1988) 11.

68. Quoted in Tom LeClair, "An Interview with Don DeLillo," *Anything Can Happen: Interviews with Contemporary American Novelists,* ed. Tom LeClair and Larry McCaffery (Urbana: University of Illinois Press, 1983) 82.

69. Bryant, "Discussing the Untellable" 25.

70. Ihab Hassan, "The Aura of a New Man," *Salmagundi* 67 (1985): 165–66.

71. William Kennedy, *Legs* (New York: Viking Penguin, 1975) 13.

72. Kennedy, *Legs* 16.

73. John Barth, *The Sot-Weed Factor* (New York: Doubleday, 1960).

CHAPTER FOUR

1. Quoted in Larry McCaffery, "Form, Formula, and Fantasy: Generative Structures in Contemporary Fiction," *Bridges to Fantasy,* ed. George E. Slusser, Eric S. Rabkin, and Robert Scholes (Carbondale: Southern Illinois University Press, 1982) 31.

2. Frank Kermode, *The Sense of an Ending: Studies in the Theory of Fiction* (New York: Oxford University Press, 1967) 7, 18.

3. Mark Spilka, ed., "Character as a Lost Cause," *Novel: A Forum on Fiction* 3 (1978): 197–99.

4. Raymond Federman, "Surfiction—Four Propositions in Form of an Introduction," *Surfiction: Fiction Now . . . and Tomorrow,* ed. Raymond Federman, 2nd ed. (Chicago: Swallow, 1981) 12.

5. Wylie Sypher, *Loss of the Self in Modern Literature and Art* (New York: Random House, 1962). See especially Chapter One, "The New Man as Functionary," and Chapter Eight, "The Anonymous Self: A Defensive Humanism."

6. William H. Gass, "The Concept of Character in Fiction," *Fiction and the Figures of Life* (Boston: David R. Godine, 1971) 49–50.

7. Ronald Sukenick, *Out* (Chicago: Swallow, 1973) 164.

8. Christopher Lasch, *The Culture of Narcissism: American Life in an Age of Diminishing Expectations* (New York: Warner, 1979) 18.

9. John Ashbery, "The Wrong Kind of Insurance," *Houseboat Days* (New York: Viking, 1977) 50.

10. Gabriel Josipovici, *The World and the Book: A Study of Modern Fiction* (Stanford, CA: Stanford University Press, 1971) 299.

11. Thomas Pynchon, *The Crying of Lot 49* (Philadelphia: J. B. Lippincott, 1966) 128.

12. Josipovici, *The World and the Book* 192–93.

13. Alain Robbe-Grillet, "A Future for the Novel," *For a New Novel: Essays on Fiction,* trans. Richard Howard (New York: Grove, 1965) 19.

14. Robbe-Grillet, "Nature, Humanism, Tragedy," *For a New Novel* 67.

15. Quoted in Claude Richard, "Causation, Causality and Etiology: A Meditation on 'Two Meditations,'" *Representation and Performance in Postmodern Fiction*, ed. Maurice Couturier (Paris: Delta, 1982) 9.

16. Quoted in Michael Holquist, "Whodunit and Other Questions: Metaphysical Detective Stories in Post-War Fiction," *New Literary History* 3 (1971): 144.

17. Steven Weisenberger, Afterword to *Accident*, by Nicholas Mosley (Elmwood Park, IL: Dalkey Archive, 1966) 197.

18. Paul Auster, *City of Glass* (New York: Penguin, 1986); *Ghosts* (New York: Penguin, 1987); *The Locked Room* (New York: Penguin, 1987). Further page references to these books appear parenthetically in the text.

19. William V. Spanos, "The Detective and the Boundary: Some Notes on the Postmodern Literary Imagination," *Boundary* 2 1 (1972): 150.

20. T. S. Eliot, *East Coker, The Complete Poems and Plays 1909–1950* (New York: Harcourt, Brace & World, 1971) 128.

21. Samuel Beckett, *Molloy, Three Novels by Samuel Beckett*, trans. Samuel Beckett and Patrick Bowles (New York: Grove, 1958) 170.

22. Beckett, *Molloy* 176.

23. See my discussion of this issue as it pertains to postmodern fiction in "Wording a World," the Introduction to *The Fiction of William Gass: The Consolation of Language* (Carbondale: Southern Illinois University Press, 1986) 6–10.

24. Thomas Docherty, *Reading (Absent) Character: Towards a Theory of Characterization in Fiction* (New York: Oxford University Press, 1983) 12–15.

25. Witold Gombrowicz, *Cosmos*, Chapters 1 and 2 in *Fiction of the Absurd: Pratfalls in the Void*, ed. Dick Penner (New York: New American Library, 1980) 163.

26. The predicament of perception, as well as the inescapability of self-perception, is ingeniously depicted in Samuel Beckett's *Film* (produced in 1964 and starring Buster Keaton), a twenty four-minute experiment on the subjection of "I" to "eye."

27. Letter to Max Brod, 5 July 1922, *I Am a Memory Come Alive: Autobiographical Writings by Franz Kafka*, ed. Nahum N. Glatzer (New York: Schocken, 1974) 223.

28. Franz Kafka, *I Am a Memory Come Alive* 21. Kafka's diaries also substantiate the corrosive solipsism that Blue endures:

I am more and more unable to think, to observe, to determine the truth of things, to remember, to speak, to share an experience; I am turning to stone, this is the truth. I am more and more unable even in the office. If I can't take refuge in some work, I am lost. (115)

29. Flann O'Brien, *At Swim-Two-Birds* (New York: New American Library, 1976) 32.

30. O'Brien, *At Swim-Two-Birds* 32.

31. It is sobering to contrast this narrator's lack of faith in explicability with the abiding, categorical faith in his task of a more accomplished literary biographer:

And yet the writer of biography must be neat and orderly and logical in describing this elusive flamelike human spirit which delights in defying order

and neatness and logic. This biographer may be as imaginative as he pleases—
the more imaginative the better—in the way in which he brings together his
materials, *but he must not imagine the materials*. He must read himself into the
past; but he must also read that past into the present. He must judge the facts,
but he must not sit in judgment. He must respect the dead—but he must tell the
truth.

Leon Edel, *Literary Biography* (Garden City, NY: Doubleday, 1959) 1–2.

32. Vladimir Nabokov, *Lolita* (New York: Putnam's, 1958); James Purdy, *Cabot Wright Begins* (New York: Farrar, Straus, and Cudahy, 1959).

33. Thomas Berger, *Who Is Teddy Villanova?* (New York: Dell, 1977). Further page references to this novel are noted parenthetically in the text.

34. Philip Kuberski, "The *Kraft* of Fiction: Nomenclatural Vandalism in *Who Is Teddy Villanova?*," *Studies in American Humor* 2.2 (1983): 12.

35. Thomas Berger, *Killing Time* (New York: Dial, 1967) 360. Further page references to this novel are noted parenthetically in the text.

36. Mircea Eliade, *Myth and Reality*, trans. Willard R. Trask (New York: Harper & Row, 1963) 193.

37. Alan Wilde, *Middle Grounds: Studies in Contemporary American Fiction* (Philadelphia: University of Pennsylvania Press, 1987) 46.

38. Wilde, *Middle Grounds* 47.

39. Leonard Michaels, "Fingers and Toes," *Going Places* (New York: Farrar, Straus & Giroux, 1969) 126.

40. Gilbert Sorrentino, "Poetic Closure," *Coherence*, ed. Don Wellman (Cambridge, MA: Alpine, 1981) 25.

41. Sorrentino, "Poetic Closure" 25.

42. Julian Cowley, "A Disintegrating Song: The Fiction of Steve Katz," *Critique: Studies in Modern Fiction* 27 (1986): 136.

43. Quoted in Larry McCaffery, "An Interview with Steve Katz," *Anything Can Happen: Interviews with Contemporary American Novelists*, ed. Tom LeClair and Larry McCaffery (Urbana: University of Illinois Press, 1983) 232–33.

44. Steve Katz, *SAW* (New York: Knopf, 1973) n.p.

45. Steve Katz, *Moving Parts* (New York: Fiction Collective, 1977) 5. Further page references to this novel are noted parenthetically in the text. Each of the four sections of the book—"Female Skin," "Parcel of Wrists," "Trip," and "43"—are separately paginated, so section titles accompany page references whenever necessary.

46. William Gass also notoriously exploits, and seemingly exhausts, the tensions between literary and sexual performance/possession in his *Willie Masters' Lonesome Wife* (*TriQuarterly Supplement 2*, Evanston, IL: Northwestern University Press, 1971).

47. Steve Katz, *The Exaggggerations of Peter Prince* (New York: Holt, Rinehart and Winston, 1968) 136.

48. Jerome Klinkowitz, *Literary Disruptions: The Making of a Post-Contemporary American Fiction*, 2nd ed. (Urbana: University of Illinois Press, 1980) 226.

49. Steve Katz, *Wier and Pouce* (College Park, MD: Sun & Moon, 1984) 29.

50. J. Kerry Grant, "Fiction and the Facts of Life," *Critique: Studies in Modern Fiction* 24 (1983): 211.

51. Cowley, "A Disintegrating Song" 141.

52. Franz Kafka, "Conversation with the Supplicant," *The Penal Colony: Stories and Short Pieces,* trans. Willa and Edwin Muir (New York: Schocken, 1976) 14.

53. William H. Gass, "The Leading Edge of the Trash Phenomenon," *Fiction and the Figures of Life* 100–101.

54. Stanley Elkin, "What's in a Name?" *Facing Texts: Encounters Between Contemporary Writers and Critics,* ed. Heide Ziegler (Durham, NC: Duke University Press, 1988) 31. Elkin's characterization of God in *The Living End* (New York: Dutton, 1979) echoes these sentiments on a divine scale when He explains that the litmus test of all Creation is what makes a better story!

55. Frederick R. Karl, *American Fictions 1940–1980: A Comprehensive History and Critical Evaluation* (New York: Harper & Row, 1983) 379.

56. Don DeLillo, *Libra* (New York: Viking, 1988) 181.

57. Joseph McElroy, *Hind's Kidnap* (New York: Harper & Row, 1969) 80.

58. Donald Barthelme, "Brain Damage," *City Life* (New York: Farrar, Straus & Giroux, 1970) 146.

59. Samuel Beckett, *Murphy* (New York: Grove, 1957) 168.

60. John Barth, *The End of the Road* (New York: Doubleday, 1958).

61. Ralph Waldo Emerson, "Experience," *Selected Writings of Emerson,* ed. Donald McQuade (New York: Random, 1981) 326.

62. James Purdy, *Malcolm* (New York: Farrar, Straus & Cudahy, 1959) 10. Further references to this novel are noted parenthetically in the text.

63. Peter Currie, "The Eccentric Self: Anti-Characterization and the Problem of the Subject in American Postmodernist Fiction," *Contemporary American Fiction,* ed. Malcolm Bradbury and Sigmund Ro (London: Edward Arnold, 1987) 59.

64. Quoted in Douglas N. Mount, "Authors and Editors: Jerzy Kosinski," *Publishers' Weekly* 26 April 1971: 15.

65. Jerzy Kosinski, *Being There* (New York: Harcourt Brace Jovanovich, 1970) 6. Further page references to this novel are noted parenthetically in the text.

66. Donald Barthelme, "The Glass Mountain," *Sixty Stories* (New York: Dutton, 1982) 182.

67. Samuel Beckett, *Endgame* (New York: Grove, 1958) 70.

68. Rudolph Wurlitzer, *Flats* (New York: Dutton, 1970) 67. Further page references to this novel are noted parenthetically in the text.

69. So too run the cryptic circumstances of Mark Strand's "Keeping Things Whole," which opens

In a field
I am the absence
of field.
This is
always the case.
Wherever I am
I am what is missing.

Contemporary American Literature, ed. George Perkins and Barbara Perkins (New York: Random, 1988) 953.

70. Thomas Pynchon, *Gravity's Rainbow* (New York: Viking, 1973) 3.

71. Rudolph Wurlitzer, *Nog* (New York: Random, 1969) 106.
72. Mark Strand, "Mr. and Mrs. Baby," *Mr. and Mrs. Baby and Other Stories* (New York: Knopf, 1985) 71.

CHAPTER FIVE

1. R. D. Laing, *Self and Others* (New York: Pantheon, 1969) 36.
2. John Barth, "Some Reasons Why I Tell the Stories I Tell The Way I Tell Them Rather Than Some Other Sort of Stories Some Other Way," *The Friday Book: Essays and Other Nonfiction* (New York: G. P. Putnam's Sons, 1984) 2–3.
3. To this end, William Gass provides the image of a pointing statue, stressing how our eyes do not look in the direction apparently being "referred" to, but instead travel back along the tensed arm. See "The Concept of Character in Fiction," *Fiction and the Figures of Life* (Boston: David R. Godine, 1971) 49.
4. Marshall Brown, "The Logic of Realism: A Hegelian Approach," *PMLA* 96 (1981) 225.
5. Michel Foucault, *The Order of Things: An Archaeology of the Human Sciences,* trans. Alan Sheridan (New York: Random, 1973) 300.
6. For a useful overview of this phenomenon, see John Vernon, "Language and Writing," *American Review* 22 (1975): 213–29.
7. Susan Sontag, "The Aesthetics of Silence," *Styles of Radical Will* (New York: Farrar, Straus and Giroux/Dell, 1969) 16.
8. Ronald Sukenick, "The New Tradition in Fiction," *Surfiction: Fiction Now . . . and Tomorrow,* ed. Raymond Federman (Chicago: Swallow, 1981) 45.
9. Appropriately, Sukenick confides that formal notions and challenges, rather than plotworthy events, provide the incentive for his own texts. His books begin with, and as, patterns. See Larry McCaffery, "An Interview with Ronald Sukenick," *Anything Can Happen: Interviews with Contemporary American Novelists,* ed. Tom LeClair and Larry McCaffery (Urbana: University of Illinois Press, 1983) 290.
10. Jerome Klinkowitz, *The Self-Apparent Word: Fiction as Language/Language as Fiction* (Carbondale: Southern Illinois University Press, 1984).
11. Roland Barthes, "Objective Literature," *Critical Essays,* trans. Richard Howard (Evanston, IL: Northwestern University Press, 1972) 14.
12. Charles Newman, *The Postmodern Aura: The Act of Fiction in an Age of Inflation, Salmagundi* 63–64 (1984): 91.
13. William Faulkner, *As I Lay Dying* (New York: Random, 1957) 163, 164.
14. T. S. Eliot, *Sweeney Agonistes, T. S. Eliot: The Complete Poems and Plays, 1909–1950* (New York: Harcourt, Brace & World, 1971) 83.
15. Samuel Beckett, *Murphy* (New York: Grove, 1957) 40.
16. Frederick R. Karl, *American Fictions, 1940–1980: A Comprehensive History and Critical Evaluation* (New York: Harper & Row, 1983) 412.
17. Martin Buber, *I and Thou,* trans. Walter Kaufmann (New York: Charles Scribner's Sons, 1970) 62, 92.
18. Floyd C. Watkins, *The Flesh and the Word: Eliot, Hemingway, Faulkner* (Nashville, TN: Vanderbilt University Press, 1971) 3.

19. Quoted in Leo Litwak, "Kay Boyle—Paris Wasn't Like That," *New York Times Book Review* 15 July 1984: 32.

20. Despite the confident tone of this and other similar manifestos regarding the autonomy of a work of art, many writers are less consoled by the hermetic status their works may have achieved. Not every postrealist author so blithely dismisses the absent world or feels assured that a seamless artifice won't find its resources depleted and crave the reality of others (even other real artworks). See Stephen J. Greenblatt, Preface, *Allegory and Representation: Selected Papers from the English Institute, 1979–1980,* New Series No. 5, ed. Stephen J. Greenblatt (Baltimore: Johns Hopkins University Press, 1981) xiii.

21. Quoted in Michael Finney, "Eugene Jolas, *transition,* and the Revolution of the Word," *In the Wake of the "Wake",* ed. David Hayman and Elliott Anderson (Madison: University of Wisconsin Press, 1978) 44.

22. George Steiner, "Of Nuance and Scruple," *Extraterritorial: Papers on Literature and the Language Revolution* (New York: Atheneum, 1971) 13.

23. Samuel Beckett, *Watt* (New York: Grove, 1959) 79.

24. Samuel Beckett, "fizzle 8," *Fizzles* (New York: Grove, 1976) 55–56.

25. Quoted in Caryl Emerson, "The Outer Word and Inner Speech: Bakhtin, Vygotsky, and the Internalization of Language," *Critical Inquiry* 10 (1983): 257.

26. Marshall McLuhan, *Understanding Media: The Extensions of Man* (New York: McGraw-Hill, 1964) 41.

27. Ronald Sukenick, *Long Talking Bad Condition Blues* (New York: Fiction Collective, 1979) 12.

28. Sukenick, *Long Talking Bad Condition Blues* 110–11.

29. Raymond Federman is perhaps the most exuberant (or shrillest) proponent of, to use his phrase, "this pursuit of Non-knowledge" as being fundamental to the advent of genuine (read "agnostic") art forms—art forms on perpetual patrol against literary conventions and rationalizations. See his "Surfiction—Four Propositions in Form of an Introduction" and "Fiction Today or the Pursuit of Non-Knowledge," *Surfiction: Fiction Now . . . and Tomorrow,* 2nd ed. (Chicago: Swallow, 1981) 5–15, 291–311.

30. Gilbert Sorrentino, "Writing and Writers: *Disjecta Membra,*" *Review of Contemporary Fiction* 8.3 (1988): 25, 28.

31. Donald Barthelme, "Bone Bubbles," *City Life* (New York: Farrar, Straus & Giroux, 1970) 117.

32. Donald Barthelme, "Sentence," *City Life* 114.

33. Donald Barthelme, "Comments on "Paraguay," quoted in Jerome Klinkowitz, *The Self-Apparent Word* 31–32.

34. Ronald Sukenick, "Thirteen Digressions," *In Form: Digressions on the Act of Fiction* (Carbondale: Southern Illinois University Press, 1985) 29.

35. Ronald Sukenick, "What's Your Story," *The Death of the Novel and Other Stories* (New York: Dial, 1969) 137. Further page references to this story are noted parenthetically in the text.

36. Ronald Sukenick, *98.6* (New York: Fiction Collective, 1975) 167.

37. Ronald Sukenick, "The Birds," *The Death of the Novel and Other Stories* 157.

38. Ronald Sukenick, *Out* (Chicago: Swallow, 1973) 164. Howard Nemerov

invites comparable projections in "The Blue Swallows"—that is, until the poet catches himself at his narcissism:

> Thus helplessly the mind in its brain
> Weaves up relations' spindthrift web,
> Seeing the swallows' tails as nibs
> Dipped in invisible ink, writing . . .
>
> Poor mind, what would you have them write?
> Some cabalistic history
> Whose authorship you might ascribe
> To God? Ah, poor ghost,
> You've capitalized your Self enough.

"The Blue Swallows," *The Collected Poems of Howard Nemerov* (Chicago: University of Chicago Press, 1977) 397.

39. John Hawkes, *Whistlejacket* (New York: Weidenfeld & Nicolson, 1988) 16. Further page references to this novel are noted parenthetically in the text.

40. T. S. Eliot, *Burnt Norton, T. S. Eliot: The Complete Poems and Plays, 1909–1950* 175.

41. It is instructive to compare the forensic/fetishistic qualities of photography in this novel to their exploration in Julio Cortázar's "Blow-Up," in *End of the Game and Other Stories,* trans. Paul Blackburn (New York: Random House, 1967) 114–31. No less provocative is Michael Antonioni's renowned film version (1966).

42. William Wordsworth, "The Tables Turned," *The Poetical Works of William Wordsworth,* ed. E. DeSelincourt (London: Oxford University Press, 1920) 481.

43. To pursue this notion further, beneath this level lies a ghostly image from Hawkes's 1961 novel, *The Lime Twig,* of a racehorse being hoisted from a barge at night. Scratch that surface, and we reveal the author's lifelong fascination with racehorses, as Hawkes discusses with Patrick O'Donnell in "Life and Art: An Interview with John Hawkes," *Review of Contemporary Fiction* 3.3 (1983): 114.

44. Herman Melville, *Moby-Dick,* ed. Harrison Hayford and Hershel Parker (New York: W. W. Norton, 1967) 228. Nor are photographs free of these indeterminacies. Patty Hearst is "captured" on automatic bank holdup cameras, which grind away but have no ax to grind. Is the young woman holding the submachine gun a brazen guerrilla or an anxious victim? How do we read her? Into what framing logic will the jurors maneuver her? See Allan Sekula, "Dismantling Modernism, Reinventing Documentary (Notes on the Politics of Representation)," *Massachusetts Review* 19 (1978): 863.

45. Quoted in R. H. Stacy, *Defamiliarization in Language and Literature* (Syracuse, NY: Syracuse University Press, 1977) 105.

46. Barbara Herrnstein Smith, *On the Margins of Discourse: The Relation of Literature to Language* (Chicago: University of Chicago Press, 1978) 11.

47. Keith Fort, "The Coal Shoveller," *Anti-Story: An Anthology of Experimental Fiction,* ed. Philip Stevick (New York: Free Press, 1971) 51. Fort's is but one of many "ante-stories" in the Stevick collection—fictions stuck in the starting gate.

48. Keith Fort, "The Coal Shoveller" 61.

49. Paul West offers these exemplary models in "The Fable's Manger," *Sheer*

Fiction (Kingston, NY: McPherson, 1988) 44–45. For an extensive descriptive analysis of the smorgasbord of stylistic variations in contemporary fiction, see Brian McHale, *Postmodern Fiction* (New York: Methuen, 1987), especially Chapters 7 through 12 (99–196).

50. William Gass, *Willie Masters' Lonesome Wife, TriQuarterly Supplement* 2 (Evanston, IL: Northwestern University Press, 1968), n. p. For a rehearsal of the problems attending referential status "alone down here," see Linda Hutcheon, *A Poetics of Postmodernism: History, Theory, Fiction* (New York: Routledge, 1988) 148 ff.

51. Ian Wallace, "Literature—Transparent and Opaque," *The Avant-Garde Tradition in Literature,* ed. Richard Kostelanetz (Buffalo, NY: Prometheus, 1982) 343.

CHAPTER SIX

1. Ernest Boyer, *College: The Undergraduate Experience in America* (New York: Harper and Row, 1987) 68.

2. William J. Bennett, "'To Reclaim a Legacy': Text of a Report on Humanities in Education," *Chronicle of Higher Education* 28 November 1984: 17.

3. Bennett, "Text of a Report" 21.

4. Lynne V. Cheney, "Humanities in America: Report to the President, the Congress, and the American People," *Chronicle of Higher Education* 21 September 1988: A17.

5. Cheney, "Humanities in America" A20.

6. See William K. Buckley, "The Good, the Bad, and the Ugly in Amerika's *Akadēmia,*" *Profession 88* (1988): 46–52. The two books that occasion Buckley's essay and six others in this annual publication of the Modern Language Association are Allan Bloom, *The Closing of the American Mind: How Higher Education Has Failed Democracy and Impoverished the Souls of Today's Students* (New York: Simon and Schuster, 1987); and E. D. Hirsch, Jr., *Cultural Literacy: What Every American Needs to Know* (Boston: Houghton Mifflin, 1987).

7. Richard Rorty, Keynote Address at the annual meeting of the Association of American Colleges, quoted in *Chronicle of Higher Education* 1 February 1989: B5.

8. Ihab Hassan, *The Right Promethean Fire: Imagination, Science, and Cultural Change* (Urbana: University of Illinois Press, 1980), quoted in a review by Jerome Klinkowitz in *Modern Fiction Studies* 26 (1980–81): 721. Hassan's book frequently admonishes us to distrust closure in all intellectual disciplines. He reminds us that "all human effort is in time, and time decomposes as well as consolidates" (17), and that "since the ideal of a structure of all possible structures seems unrealizable, knowledge must remain *finally indeterminate*" (102).

9. Richard Poirier, *The Renewal of Literature: Emersonian Reflections* (New York: Random House, 1987) 49. Poirier asks us to dispense with what he implies is an almost religious faith in literature as a "reclamation project," for that attitude fails to account for the emphasis of great writers of the past upon "the futility of this quest for truth, values, and exaltations" (4). Furthermore, Poirier's response to "the notion that the writing and reading of literature have a culturally redemptive power" bears precisely upon the stance I am developing here:

I am arguing that this belief cannot be sustained by the actual operations of language in literary texts. Writing that can be called literature tends, it seems to me, to be discernibly on edge about its own rhetorical status, especially when the rhetoric is conspicuously indebted to any of the great, historically rooted institutions. . . . Part of the excitement derives from the way such works resist as well as absorb the meanings which their adopted language makes available to them, and us. (9)

10. Poirier, *Renewal of Literature* 70–72. To resist the stranglehold of inherited culture and language on consciousness, Poirier argues, we can "effectively register our dissent . . . by means of troping, punning, parodistic echoings, and by letting vernacular idioms play against revered terminologies" (72). Chapter Five of this study offer parallels to these stylistic strategies as they relate to more recent literature.

11. T. S. Eliot, *Burnt Norton, The Complete Poems and Plays, 1909–1950* (New York: Harcourt, Brace & World, 1971) 119.

12. Timothy Bahti, "Ambiguity and Indeterminacy: The Juncture," *Comparative Literature* 38 (1986): 211–13.

13. Bahti, "Ambiguity" 210.

14. Howard Nemerov, *Journal of the Fictive Life* (Chicago: University of Chicago Press, 1981) 105.

15. Wayne C. Booth, *The Company We Keep: An Ethics of Fiction* (Berkeley: University of California Press, 1988) 62 ff. Booth also explains that, paradoxically, even the claim that openness and arbitrariness are the inevitable conditions of contemporary art, however unrestrictive it may appear on the surface, also smacks of absolutism; it, too, is a prejudice that must be suspended so as not to contaminate an inquiry into where value inheres in literature.

16. Patrick O'Donnell, *Passionate Doubts: Designs of Interpretation in Contemporary American Fiction* (Iowa City: University of Iowa Press, 1986) 158.

17. Quoted in Philip and Phylis Morrison, *The Ring of Truth: An Inquiry into How We Know What We Know* (New York: Random House, 1987) 262.

18. Don DeLillo, *White Noise* (New York: Viking, 1985) 324–25.

Bibliography

Abish, Walter, *Alphabetical Africa*. New York: New Directions, 1974.
———. "The English Garden." *In the Future Perfect*. New York: New Directions, 1977. 1–21.
———. "The Fall of Summer." *Conjunctions* 7 (Summer 1984): 110–41.
———. *How German Is It*. New York: New Directions, 1980.
Adler, Renata. *Speedboat*. New York: Random House, 1976.
Aldridge, John. *The American Novel and the Way We Live Now*. New York: Oxford University Press, 1983.
Alter, Robert. "Mimesis and the Motive for Fiction." *TriQuarterly* 42 (1978): 228–49.
Arendt, Hannah. *The Origins of Totalitarianism*. New Edition. New York: Harcourt Brace Jovanovich, 1966.
Ashbery, John. "The Wrong Kind of Insurance." *Houseboat Days*. New York: Viking, 1977. 50.
Auster, Paul. *City of Glass*. New York: Penguin, 1986.
———. *Ghosts*. New York: Penguin, 1987.
———. *The Locked Room*. New York: Penguin, 1987.
Bahti, Timothy. "Ambiguity and Indeterminacy: The Juncture." *Comparative Literature* 38 (1986): 209–23.
Barth, John. *The End of the Road*. New York: Doubleday, 1958.
———. *LETTERS*. New York: G. P. Putnam's Sons, 1979.
———. "The Literature of Exhaustion." 1967; rpt. *The American Novel Since World War II*. Ed. Marcus Klein. New York: Fawcett, 1969. 267–79.
———. "Some Reasons Why I Tell the Stories I Tell the Way I Tell Them Rather Than Some Other Sort of Stories Some Other Way." *The Friday Book: Essays and Other Nonfiction*. New York: G. P. Putnam's Sons, 1984. 1–12.
———. *The Sot-Weed Factor*. New York: Doubleday, 1960.
Barthelme, Donald. *City Life*. New York: Farrar, Straus & Giroux, 1970.
———. "Not-Knowing." *Voice-Lust: Eight Contemporary Fiction Writers on Style*. Ed. Allen Wier and Don Hendrie, Jr. Lincoln: University of Nebraska Press, 1985, 37–50.
———. *Sixty Stories*. New York: Dutton, 1982.
———. *Snow White*. New York: Atheneum, 1967.
Barthes, Roland. "Objective Literature." *Critical Essays*. Trans. Richard Howard. Evanston, IL: Northwestern University Press, 1972. 13–24.
Bawer, Bruce. *Diminishing Fictions: Essays on the Modern American Novel and Its Critics*. St. Paul, MN: Graywolf, 1988.
Beckett, Samuel. *Endgame*. New York: Grove, 1958.
———. "fizzle 8." *Fizzles*. New York: Grove, 1976. 55–61.
———. "Imagination Dead Imagine." *First Love and Other Shorts*. New York· Grove, 1974. 61–66

————. *Murphy*. New York: Grove, 1957.

————. *Ohio Impromptu. Rockaby and Other Short Pieces*. New York: Grove, 1981. 25–35.

————. *Three Novels: Molloy, Malone Dies, The Unnamable*. New York: Grove, 1958.

————. *Waiting for Godot*. New York: Grove, 1954.

————. *Watt*. New York: Grove, 1959.

Beja, Morris. *Epiphany in the Modern Novel*. Seattle: University of Washington Press, 1971.

Bellamy, Joe David. *The New Fiction: Interviews with Innovative American Writers*. Urbana: University of Illinois Press, 1974.

————, ed. *Moral Fiction: An Anthology*. Canton, NY: Fiction International, 1980.

Bellow, Saul. *Mr. Sammler's Planet*. New York: Viking, 1970.

Benamou, Michel, and Charles Caramello, eds. *Performance in Postmodern Culture*. Madison, WI: Coda, 1977.

Bennett, William J. "'To Reclaim a Legacy': Text of a Report on Humanities in Education." *Chronicle of Higher Education* 28 November 1984: 16–21.

Berger, Thomas. *Killing Time*. New York: Dial, 1967.

————. *Who Is Teddy Villanova?* New York: Dell, 1977.

Bloom, Allan. *The Closing of the American Mind: Education and the Crisis of Reason*. New York: Simon & Schuster, 1987.

Booth, Wayne C. *The Company We Keep: An Ethics of Fiction*. Berkeley: University of California Press, 1988.

Borges, Jorge Luis. *Labyrinths: Selected Stories and Other Writings*. Ed. Donald A. Yates and James E. Irby. New York: New Directions, 1964.

Boyer, Ernest. *College: The Undergraduate Experience in America*. New York: Harper & Row, 1987.

Bradbury, Malcolm. "Modernisms/Postmodernisms." Hassan and Hassan 311–27.

Brown, Marshall. "The Logic of Realism: A Hegelian Approach." *PMLA* 96 (1981): 224–41.

Bryant, Jerry H. *The Open Decision: The Contemporary American Novel and Its Intellectual Background*. New York: Free Press, 1970.

Bryant, Paula. "Discussing the Untellable: Don DeLillo's *The Names*." *Critique* 29 (1987): 16–29.

Buber, Martin. *I and Thou*. Trans. Walter Kaufmann. New York: Charles Scribner's Sons, 1970.

Buckley, William K. "The Good, the Bad, and the Ugly in Amerika's *Akadēmia*." *Profession 88* (1988): 46–52.

Bulhof, Ilse N. "Imagination and Interpretation in History." *Literature and History*. Ed. Leonard Schulze and Walter Wetzels. Lanham, MD: University Press of America, 1983, 3–25.

Butler, Christopher. "Scepticism and Experimental Fiction." *Essays in Criticism* 36 (1986): 47–67.

Calvino, Italo. *Cosmicomics*. Trans. William Weaver. New York: Harcourt Brace Jovanovich, 1968.

Camus, Albert. *The Plague*. Trans. Stuart Gilbert. New York: Alfred A. Knopf, 1948.

Canary, Robert H., and Henry Kozicki. *The Writing of History: Literary Form and Historical Understanding*. Madison: University of Wisconsin Press, 1978.

Caramello, Charles. *Silverless Mirrors: Book, Self & Postmodern American Fiction*. Tallahassee: University Presses of Florida, 1983.

Chabot, C. Barry. "The Problem of the Postmodern." *New Literary History* 20 (1988): 1–20.

Cheney, Lynne V. *Humanities in America: A Report to the President, the Congress, and the American People*. Washington, D.C.: National Endowment for the Humanities, 1988.

Clayton, John. "Radical Jewish Humanism." Trenner 109–19.

Clemens, Samuel Langhorne. *Adventures of Huckleberry Finn*. Ed. Sculley Bradley, Richmond Groom Beatty, and E. Hudson Long. New York: W. W. Norton, 1962.

Coover, Robert. *Gerald's Party*. Interlaken, NY: Linden, 1986.

——. *Pricksongs and Descants*. New York: Dutton, 1969.

——. *Spanking the Maid*. New York: Grove, 1982.

——. *Whatever Happened to Gloomy Gus of the Chicago Bears?* Interlaken, NY: Linden, 1987.

Cope, Jackson I., and Geoffrey Green, eds. *Novel vs. Fiction: The Contemporary Reformation*. Special issue of *Genre* 14.1 (1981).

Cornis-Pop, Marcel. "Working Theories of New Fiction." *North American Review* 270 (September 1985): 66–70.

Cortazar, Julio. "Blow-Up." *End of the Game and Other Stories*. Trans. Paul Blackburn. New York: Random House, 1967. 114–31.

Cowley, Julian. "A Disintegrating Song: The Fiction of Steve Katz." *Critique* 27 (1986): 131–43.

Cummings, E. E. "pity this busy monster." *Complete Poems, 1913–1962*. New York: Harcourt Brace Jovanovich, 1972. 554.

Currie, Peter. "The Eccentric Self: Anti-Characterization and the Problem of the Subject in American Postmodernist Fiction." *Contemporary American Fiction*. Ed. Malcolm Bradbury and Sigmund Ro. London: Edward Arnold, 1987. 52–69.

DeLillo, Don. *Libra*. New York: Viking, 1988.

——. *The Names*. New York: Random House, 1982.

——. *Ratner's Star*. New York: Random House, 1980.

——. *White Noise*. New York: Viking, 1985.

Ditsky, John M. "The Man on the Quaker Oats Box: Characteristics of Recent Experimental Fiction." *Georgia Review* 26 (1972): 297–313.

Docherty, Thomas. *Reading (Absent) Character: Towards a Theory of Characterization in Fiction*. New York: Oxford University Press, 1983.

Doctorow, E. L. *Big as Life*. New York: Simon and Schuster, 1966.

——. *The Book of Daniel*. New York: Random House, 1971.

——. "False Documents." Trenner 16–27.

——. "The Foreign Legation." *Lives of the Poets*. New York: Random House, 1984. 53–63.

——. *Ragtime*. New York: Random House, 1975.

——. *Welcome to Hard Times*. New York: Simon and Schuster, 1960.

Edel, Leon. *Literary Biography.* Garden City, NY: Doubleday, 1959.

Edelman, Murray. "Political Language and Political Reality." *PS: Political Science and Politics* 18.1 (10): 10–19.

Edmundson, Mark. "Prophet of a New Postmodernism: The Greater Challenge of Salman Rushdie." *Harper's* December 1989: 62–71.

Eliade, Mircea. *Myth and Reality.* Trans. Willard R. Trask. New York: Harper & Row, 1963.

Eliot. T. S. *Selected Prose.* Ed. Frank Kermode. New York: Harcourt Brace Jovanovich, 1975.

———. *T. S. Eliot: The Complete Poems and Plays, 1909–1950.* New York: Harcourt, Brace, 1971.

Elkin, Stanley. *The Living End.* New York: Dutton, 1979.

———. "What's in a Name?" *Facing Texts: Encounters Between Contemporary Writers and Critics.* Ed. Heide Ziegler. Durham, NC: Duke University Press, 1988. 17–31.

Emerson, Caryl. "The Outer Word and Inner Speech: Bakhtin, Vygotsky, and the Internalization of Language." *Critical Inquiry* 10 (1983): 245–64.

Emerson, Ralph Waldo. "Experience." *Selected Writings of Emerson.* Ed. Donald McQuade. New York: Random, 1981. 326–48.

Erwin, Robert. "The Great Language Panic." *Antioch Review* 45 (1987): 421–34.

Faulkner, William. *As I Lay Dying.* New York: Random House, 1957.

———. *The Sound and the Fury.* New York: Random House, 1973.

Federman, Raymond. *Take It or Leave It.* New York: Fiction Collective, 1976.

———, ed. *Surfiction: Fiction Now . . . and Tomorrow.* 2nd ed. Chicago: Swallow, 1981.

Finney, Michael. "Eugene Jolas, *transition,* and the Revolution of the Word." *In the Wake of the "Wake."* Ed. David Hayman and Elliott Anderson. Madison: University of Wisconsin Press, 1978. 39–53.

Fogel, Stanley. "'And All the Little Typtopies': Notes on Language Theory in the Contemporary Experimental Novel." *Modern Fiction Studies* 20 (1974): 328–36.

Fort, Keith. "The Coal Shoveller." *Anti-Story: An Anthology of Experimental Fiction.* Ed. Philip Stevick. New York: Free Press, 1971. 40–61.

Foucault, Michel. *The Archaeology of Knowledge.* Trans. Rupert Swyer. New York: Pantheon, 1971.

———. *The Order of Things: An Archaeology of the Human Sciences.* Trans. Alan Sheridan. New York: Random House, 1973.

Friedman, Alan. *The Turn of the Novel.* New York: Oxford University Press, 1966.

Frost, Robert. *The Poetry of Robert Frost.* Ed. Edward Connery Lathem. New York: Holt, Rinehart and Winston, 1969.

Gaddis, William. *The Recognitions.* New York: Harcourt, Brace, 1955.

Gangemi, Kenneth, *OLT.* New York: Marion Boyars, 1984.

Gardner, John. *Grendel.* New York: Random House, 1975.

———. *On Moral Fiction.* New York: Basic, 1978.

Gass, William H. *Fiction and the Figures of Life.* Boston: David R. Godine, 1971.

———. Foreword to *The Franchiser.* By Stanley Elkin (1976). Boston: David R. Godine, 1980. vii–xv.

———. *Habitations of the Word: Essays*. New York: Simon and Schuster, 1985.

———. *Willie Masters' Lonesome Wife*. *TriQuarterly Supplement 2*. Evanston, IL: Northwestern University Press, 1968.

———. *The World Within the Word*. New York: Alfred A. Knopf, 1978.

Gerlach, John. *Toward the End: Closure and Structure in the American Short Story*. University: University of Alabama Press, 1985.

Gitlin, Todd. "Hip-Deep in Postmodernism." *New York Times Book Review* 6 November 1988: 1, 35–36.

Gombrowicz, Witold. *Cosmos*, Chapters 1 and 2. *Fiction of the Absurd: Pratfalls in the Void*. Ed. Dick Penner. New York: New American Library, 1980. 139–66.

Gossman, Lionel. "History and Literature: Reproduction or Signification." Canary and Kozicki 3–40.

Graff, Gerald. *Literature Against Itself: Literary Ideas in Modern Society*. Chicago: University of Chicago Press, 1979.

Grant, J. Kerry. "Fiction and the Facts of Life." *Critique* 24 (1983): 206–13.

Greenblatt, Stephen J., ed. *Allegory and Representation: Selected Papers from the English Institute, 1979–1980*. New Series No. 5. Baltimore: Johns Hopkins University Press, 1981.

Greenman, Myron. "Understanding New Fiction." *Modern Fiction Studies* 20 (1974): 307–16.

Guerard, Albert J. "Notes on the Rhetoric of Anti-Realist Fiction." *TriQuarterly* 30 (1974): 3–50.

Gura, Philip F. "Language and Meaning: An American Tradition." *American Literature* 53 (1981): 1–21.

Hansen, Arlen J. "The Celebration of Solipsism: A New Trend in American Fiction." *Modern Fiction Studies* 19 (1973): 5–15.

Harpham, Geoffrey Galt. "E. L. Doctorow and the Technology of Narrative." *PMLA* 100 (1985): 81–95.

Hassan, Ihab. "The Aura of a New Man." *Salmagundi* 67 (1985): 163–70.

———. *The Right Promethean Fire: Imagination, Science, and Cultural Change*. Urbana: University of Illinois Press, 1980.

Hassan, Ihab, and Sally Hassan, eds. *Innovation/Renovation: New Perspectives on the Humanities*. Madison: University of Wisconsin Press, 1983.

Hawkes, John. *The Lime Twig*. New York: New Directions, 1961.

———. "Notes on Writing a Novel." *TriQuarterly* 30 (1974): 109–26.

———. *Whistlejacket*. New York: Weidenfeld & Nicolson, 1988.

Hawthorne, Nathaniel. *Fanshawe. The Centenary Edition of the Works of Nathaniel Hawthorne*. Vol. 3. Ed. William Charvat et al. Columbus: Ohio State University Press, 1964.

———. "Wakefield." *Twice-Told Tales. The Centenary Edition of the Works of Nathaniel Hawthorne*. Vol. 9. 130–40.

Hayles, Kathryn. *The Cosmic Web: Scientific Models and Literary Strategies in the Twentieth Century*. Ithaca, NY: Cornell University Press, 1984.

Hayman, David. *Re-Forming the Narrative: Toward a Mechanics of Modernist Fiction*. Ithaca, NY: Cornell University Press, 1987.

Heller, Joseph. *Catch-22*. New York: Simon and Schuster, 1961.

Hexter, J. M. *Doing History*. Bloomington: Indiana University Press, 1971.

Hirsch, Jr., E. D. *Cultural Literacy: What Every American Needs to Know.* Boston: Houghton Mifflin, 1987.

Hite, Molly. *Ideas of Order in the Novels of Thomas Pynchon.* Columbus: Ohio State University Press, 1983.

Holquist, Michael. "Whodunit and Other Questions: Metaphysical Detective Stories in Post-War Fiction." *New Literary History* 3 (1971): 135–56.

Hume, Kathryn. *Fantasy and Mimesis: Responses to Reality in Western Literature.* New York: Methuen, 1984.

Hutcheon, Linda. *A Poetics of Postmodernism: History, Theory, Fiction.* New York: Routledge, 1988.

Jefferson, Ann. "Structuralism and Post-Structuralism." *Modern Literary Theory: A Comparative Introduction.* Ed. A. J. and David Roby. Totowa, NJ: Barnes & Noble, 1982. 84–112.

Josipovici, Gabriel. *The World and the Book: A Study of Modern Fiction.* Stanford, CA: Stanford University Press, 1971.

Joyce, James. *A Portrait of the Artist as a Young Man.* Ed. Chester G. Anderson. New York: Viking, 1968.

———. *Ulysses.* New York: Modern Library, 1946.

Kafka, Franz. "Conversation with the Supplicant." *The Penal Colony: Stories and Short Pieces.* Trans. Willa and Edwin Muir. New York: Schocken, 1976. 9–17.

———. *I Am a Memory Come Alive: Autobiographical Writings by Franz Kafka.* Ed. Nahum N. Glatzer. New York: Schocken, 1974.

———. *The Metamorphosis.* Trans. A. L. Lloyd. New York: Vanguard, 1946.

Karl, Frederick R. *American Fictions, 1940–1980: A Comprehensive History and Critical Evaluation.* New York: Harper & Row, 1983.

Katz, Steve. *The Exagggerations of Peter Prince.* New York: Holt, Rinehart and Winston, 1968.

———. *Moving Parts.* New York: Fiction Collective, 1977.

———. *SAW.* New York: Knopf, 1973.

———. *Wier and Pouce.* College Park, MD: Sun & Moon, 1984.

Kazin, Alfred. *An American Procession: The Major American Writers from 1830 to 1930—The Crucial Century.* New York: Alfred A. Knopf, 1984.

Kennedy, William. *Legs.* New York: Viking/Penguin, 1975.

Kermode, Frank. *The Sense of an Ending: Studies in the Theory of Fiction.* New York: Oxford University Press, 1967.

Klinkowitz, Jerome. *Literary Disruptions: The Making of a Post-Contemporary American Fiction.* 2nd ed. Urbana: University of Illinois Press, 1980.

———. *The Self-Apparent Word: Fiction as Language/Language as Fiction.* Carbondale: Southern Illinois University Press, 1984.

Kosinski, Jerzy. *Being There.* New York: Harcourt Brace Jovanovich, 1970.

———. *Steps.* New York: Random House, 1968.

Kostelanetz, Richard. "Constructivist Fiction." *Chicago Review* 28 (1976): 138–41.

Kuberski, Philip. "The *Kraft* of Fiction: Nonemclatural Vandalism in *Who Is Teddy Villanova?*" *Studies in American Humor* 2.2 (1983): 117–29.

Kutnik, Jerzy. *The Novel as Performance: The Fiction of Ronald Sukenick and Raymond Federman.* Carbondale: Southern Illinois University Press, 1986.

LaCapra, Dominick. "Intellectual History and Defining the Present as 'Postmodern.'" Hassan and Hassan 47–63.

Laing, R. D. *Self and Others*. New York: Pantheon, 1969.

Lasch, Christopher. *The Culture of Narcissism: American Life in an Age of Diminishing Expectations*. New York: Warner, 1979.

Lauzen, Sarah E. "Men Wearing Macintoshes, the Macguffin in the Carpet, (Aunt Martha—*still?*—on the Stair)." *Chicago Review* 33.3 (1983): 57–77.

———, ed. *Is the Text Opaque?* Special Section of *Chicago Review* 33.2 (1982): 4–115.

LeClair, Tom. *In the Loop: Don DeLillo and the Systems Novel*. Urbana: University of Illinois Press, 1988.

———. "An Interview with Don DeLillo." LeClair and McCaffery 79–90.

LeClair, Tom, and Larry McCaffery, eds. *Anything Can Happen: Interviews with Contemporary American Novelists*. Urbana: University of Illinois Press, 1983.

Levine, Paul. "The Writer as Independent Witness." (Interview with E. L. Doctorow). Trenner 182–95.

Levitt, Morton P. *Modernist Survivors: The Contemporary Novel in England, the United States, France, and Latin America*. Columbus: Ohio State University Press, 1987.

Litwak, Leo. "Kay Boyle—Paris Wasn't Like That." *New York Times Book Review* 15 July 1984: 1, 32–33.

Logan, Robert K. *The Alphabet Effect: The Impact of the Phonetic Alphabet on the Development of Western Civilization*. New York: St. Martin's, 1986.

Lorsch, Susan E. "Doctorow's *The Book of Daniel* and *Künstlerroman:* The Politics of Art." *Papers on Language and Literature* 18 (1982): 384–97.

Malmgren, Carl Darryl. *Fictional Space in the Modernist and Postmodernist American Novel*. Lewisburg, PA: Bucknell University Press, 1985.

Martin, Richard. "Clio Bemused: The Uses of History in Contemporary American Fiction." *Sub-stance* 27 (1980): 13–24.

———. "Walter Abish's Fictions: Perfect Unfamiliarity, Familiar Imperfection." *Journal of American Studies* 17 (1983). 229–41.

Mazurek, Raymond A. "Ideology and Form in the Postmodernist Historical Novel: *The Sot-Weed Factor* and *Gravity's Rainbow*." *Minnesota Review* 25 (1985): 69–84.

McCaffery, Larry. "Form, Formula, and Fantasy: Generative Structures in Contemporary Fiction." *Bridges to Fantasy*. Ed. George E. Slusser, Eric S. Rabkin, and Robert Scholes. Carbondale: Southern Illinois University Press, 1982. 21–37.

———. "An Interview with Ronald Sukenick." LeClair and McCaffery 279–97.

———. "An Interview with Steve Katz." LeClair and McCaffery 219–34.

———. *The Metafictional Muse: The Works of Robert Coover, Donald Barthelme, and William H. Gass*. Pittsburgh: University of Pittsburgh Press, 1982.

———. "A Spirit of Transgression." (Interview with E. L. Doctorow). Trenner 31–47.

McElroy, Joseph. *Hind's Kidnap*. New York: Harper & Row, 1969.

McHale, Brian. *Postmodern Fiction*. New York: Methuen, 1987.

McLuhan, Marshall. *Understanding Media: The Extensions of Man*. New York: McGraw-Hill, 1964.

Meisel, Perry. "Imitation Modernism." *Atlantic* March 1982: 86–88.

Melville, Herman. *Moby-Dick*. Ed. Harrison Hayford and Hershel Parker. New York: W. W. Norton, 1967.

Michaels, Leonard. "Fingers and Toes." *Going Places*. New York: Farrar, Straus & Giroux, 1969. 121–41.

Miller, D. A. *Narrative and Its Discontents: Problems of Closure in the Traditional Novel*. Princeton, NJ: Princeton University Press, 1981.

Miller, J. Hillis. "Narrative and History." *ELH* 41 (1974): 455–73.

Mink, Louis O. "History and Fiction as Modes of Comprehension." *New Literary History* 1 (1970): 541–58.

———. "Narrative Form as a Cognitive Instrument." Canary and Kozicki 129–50.

Morrison, Philip, and Phylis Morrison. *The Ring of Truth: An Inquiry into How We Know What We Know*. New York: Random House, 1987.

Mount, Douglas N. "Authors and Editors: Jerzy Kosinski." *Publishers' Weekly* 26 April 1971: 15.

Murphy, John W. "Dimensions of Postmodern Culture." *Midwest Quarterly* 29 (1988): 293–307.

Nabokov, Vladimir. *Lolita*. New York: Putnam's, 1958.

Nadeau, Robert. *Readings from the New Book on Nature: Physics and Metaphysics in the Modern Novel*. Amherst: University of Massachusetts Press, 1981.

Naremore, James. "Style as Meaning in *A Portrait of the Artist*." *James Joyce Quarterly* 4 (Summer 1967): 331–42.

Nelson, Cary. *The Incarnate Word: Literature as Verbal Space*. Urbana: University of Illinois Press, 1973.

Nemerov, Howard. "The Blue Swallows." *The Collected Poems of Howard Nemerov*. Chicago: University of Chicago Press, 1977. 397.

———. *Journal of the Fictive Life*. Chicago: University of Chicago Press, 1981.

Newman, Charles. *The Post-Modern Aura: The Act of Fiction in an Age of Inflation*. *Salmagundi* 63–64 (1984): 3–199.

Nichols, Ashton. *The Poetics of Epiphany: Nineteenth-Century Origins of the Modern Literary Movement*. Tuscaloosa: University of Alabama Press, 1987.

O'Brien, Flann. *At Swim-Two-Birds*. New York: New American Library, 1976.

O'Brien, John. "Third Degree." *American Book Review* 8 (May–June 1986): 11.

O'Donnell, Patrick. "Life and Art: An Interview with John Hawkes." *Review of Contemporary Fiction* 3.3 (1983): 107–26.

———. *Passionate Doubts: Designs of Interpretation in Contemporary American Fiction*. Iowa City: Iowa University Press, 1986.

Onopa, Robert. "The End of Art as a Spiritual Project." *TriQuarterly* 26 (Winter 1973): 363–82.

Orr, Linda. "The Revenge of Literature: The History of History." *New Literary History* 18 (1986): 1–22.

Ortega y Gasset, José. *The Dehumanization of Art*. Garden City, NY: Doubleday, 1956.

Ozick, Cynthia. "The Muse, Postmodern and Homeless." *New York Times Book Review* 18 January 1987: 9.

Paley, Grace. "A Conversation with My Father." *Enormous Changes at the Last Minute*. New York: Farrar, Straus and Giroux, 1974. 159–67.

Parks, John G. "Human Destiny and Contemporary Narrative Form." *Western Humanities Review* 38 (1984): 99–107.

Pearce, Richard. *The Novel in Motion: An Approach to Fiction*. Columbus: Ohio State University Press, 1983.

Peckham, Morse. *Man's Rage for Chaos: Biology, Behavior, and the Arts*. Philadelphia: Chilton, 1965.

Poirier, Richard. *The Performing Self: Compositions and Decompositions in the Languages of Contemporary Life*. New York: Oxford University Press, 1971.

———. "The Politics of Self-Parody." *Partisan Review* 35 (1968): 339–53.

———. *The Renewal of Literature: Emersonian Reflections*. New York: Random House, 1987.

Price, Martin. "The Irrelevant Detail and the Emergence of Form." *Aspects of Narrative: Selected Papers from the English Institute*. Ed. J. Hillis Miller. New York: Columbia University Press, 1971. 69–91.

———. "The Other Self: Thoughts About Character in the Novel." *Imagined Worlds: Essays on Some English Novels and Novelists in Honour of John Butt*. Ed. Maynard Mack and Ian Gregor. London: Methuen, 1968. 279–99.

Purdy, James. *Cabot Wright Begins*. New York: Farrar, Straus, and Cudahy, 1959.

———. *Malcolm*. New York: Farrar, Straus and Cudahy, 1959.

Putz, Manfred. *The Story of Identity: American Fiction of the Sixties*. Stuttgart: Metzler, 1979.

Pynchon, Thomas. *The Crying of Lot 49*. Philadelphia: J. B. Lippincott, 1966.

———. *Gravity's Rainbow*. New York: Viking, 1973.

———. *V*. Philadelphia: J. B. Lippincott, 1963.

Richard, Claud. "Causality and Mimesis in Contemporary Fiction." *Substance* 40 (1983): 84–93.

———. "Causation, Causality and Etiology: A Meditation on 'Two Meditations.'" *Representation and Performance in Postmodern Fiction*. Ed. Maurice Couturier. Paris: Delta, 1982. 9–20.

Robbe-Grillet, Alain. *For a New Novel: Essays on Fiction*. Trans. Richard Howard. New York: Grove, 1965.

Robbins, Bruce. "Modernism in History, Modernism in Power." *Modernism Reconsidered*. Harvard English Studies 11. Ed. Robert Kiely and John Hildebidle. Cambridge, MA: Harvard University Press, 1983. 229–45.

Rorty, Richard. Keynote Address, Association of American Colleges. Excerpt in *The Chronicle of Higher Education* 1 February 1989: B5.

Roth, Philip. "Writing American Fiction." 1961; rpt. *The Novel Today: Contemporary Writers on Modern Fiction*. Ed. Malcolm Bradbury. Glasgow: William Collins Sons, 1977. 32–47.

Russell, Charles. "Individual Voice in the Collective Discourse: Literary Innovation in Postmodern American Fiction." *Sub-stance* 27 (1980): 29–39.

———. "The Vault of Language: Self-Reflective Artifice in Contemporary American Fiction." *Modern Fiction Studies* 20 (1974): 349–59.

Ryf, Robert S. "Character and Imagination in the Experimental Novel." *Modern Fiction Studies* 20 (1974): 317–27.

Saalman, Dieter. "Walter Abish's *How German Is It*: Language and the Crisis of Human Behavior." *Critique* 26 (1985): 105–21.

Saltzman, Arthur M. *The Fiction of William Gass: The Consolation of Language*. Carbondale: Southern Illinois University Press, 1986.

Sandro, Paul. "The Management of Destiny in Narrative Form." *Cine-Tracts* 4.1 (1981): 50–56.

Seamon, Roger G. "Narrative Practice and the Theoretical Distinction between History and Fiction." *Genre* 16 (1983): 197–218.

Sekula, Allan. "Dismantling Modernism, Reinventing Documentary (Notes on the Politics of Representation)." *Massachusetts Review* 19 (1978): 859–83.

Sidney, Sir Philip. "The Defense of Poesy." *Sir Philip Sidney's Defense of Poesy*. Ed. Lewis Soens. Lincoln: University of Nebraska Press, 1970.

Silliman, Ron. *Ketjak*. San Francisco: This Press, 1978.

Singer, Isaac Bashevis. "Gimpel the Fool." *Contemporary American Fiction*. Ed. George and Barbara Perkins. New York: Random House, 1988. 26–35.

Smith, Barbara Herrnstein. *On the Margins of Discourse: The Relation of Literature to Language*. Chicago: University of Chicago Press, 1978.

Smitten, Jeffrey R., and Ann Daghistany. *Spatial Form in Narrative*. Ithaca, NY: Cornell University Press, 1981.

Sontag, Susan. "The Aesthetics of Silence." *Styles of Radical Will*. New York: Farrar, Straus and Giroux, 1969. 3–34.

———. *Against Interpretation and Other Essays*. New York: Farrar, Straus and Giroux, 1966.

Sorrentino, Gilbert. *Imaginative Qualities of Actual Things*. New York: Pantheon, 1971.

———. "Language—Lying and Treacherous." *New York Times Book Review* 25 May 1986: 23.

———. *Mulligan Stew*. New York: Grove, 1979.

———. *Odd Number*. San Francisco: North Point, 1985.

———. "Poetic Closure." *Coherence*. Ed. Don Wellman. Cambridge, MA: Alpine, 1981. 25.

———. "Writing and Writers: *Disjecta Membra*." *Review of Contemporary Fiction* 8.3 (1988): 25–35.

Spanos, William V. "The Detective and the Boundary: Some Notes on the Postmodern Literary Imagination." *Boundary 2* 2 (Fall 1972): 147–68.

Spencer, Sharon. *Space, Time and Structure in the Modern Novel*. New York: New York University Press, 1971.

Spilka, Mark, ed. "Character as a Lost Cause." *Novel: A Forum on Fiction* 3 (1978): 197–217.

Stacy, R. H. *Defamiliarization in Language and Literature*. Syracuse, NY: Syracuse University Press, 1977.

Steiner, George. *Language and Silence: Essays on Language, Literature, and the Inhuman*. New York: Atheneum, 1967.

———. "Of Nuance and Scruple." *Extraterritorial: Papers on Literature and the Language Revolution*. New York: Atheneum, 1971. 12–21.

Stevens, Wallace. *The Collected Poems of Wallace Stevens*. New York: Random House, 1954.

Stevick, Philip. *Alternative Pleasures: Post-Realist Fiction and the Tradition*. Urbana: University of Illinois Press, 1981.

Strand, Mark. "Keeping Things Whole." *Contemporary American Literature*. Ed. George and Barbara Perkins. New York: Random House, 1988. 953.

———. "Mr. and Mrs. Baby." *Mr. and Mrs. Baby and Other Stories*. New York: Alfred A. Knopf, 1985. 62–71.

Strout, Cushing. *The Veracious Imagination: Essays on American History, Literature, and Biography*. Middletown, CT: Wesleyan University Press, 1981.

Sukenick, Ronald. *The Death of the Novel and Other Stories*. New York: Dial, 1969.

———. *In Form: Digressions on the Act of Fiction*. Carbondale: Southern Illinois University Press, 1985.

———. *Long Talking Bad Condition Blues*. New York: Fiction Collective, 1979.

———. *98.6*. New York: Fiction Collective, 1975.

———. *Out*. Chicago: Swallow, 1973.

———. *Up*. New York: Dial, 1968.

"A Symposium on Contemporary American Fiction." *Michigan Quarterly Review* 26 (1987): 679–758; 27 (Winter 1988): 79–135.

Sypher, Wylie. *Loss of the Self in Modern Literature and Art*. New York: Random House, 1962.

Tani, Stefano. *The Doomed Detective: The Contribution of the Detective Novel to Postmodern American and Italian Fiction*. Carbondale: Southern Illinois University Press, 1984.

Tanner, Tony. *City of Words: American Fiction 1950–1970*. New York: Harper & Row, 1971.

Thiher, Allen. *Words in Reflection: Modern Language Theory and Postmodern Fiction*. Chicago: University of Chicago Press, 1984.

Torgovnick, Marianna. *Closure in the Novel*. Princeton, NJ: Princeton University Press, 1981.

Trenner, Richard, ed. *E. L. Doctorow: Essays and Conversations*. Princeton, NJ: Ontario Review Press, 1983.

Vernon, John. "Language and Writing." *New American Review* 22 (1975): 213–29.

Vonnegut, Jr., Kurt. *Cat's Cradle*. New York: Delacorte/Seymour Lawrence, 1963.

———. *Slaughterhouse-Five; or, The Children's Crusade*. New York: Delacorte/Seymour Lawrence, 1969.

Wallace, Ian. "Literature—Transparent and Opaque." *The Avant-Garde Tradition in Literature*. Ed. Richard Kostelanetz. Buffalo, NY: Prometheus, 1982. 341–43.

Watkins, Floyd C. *The Flesh and the Word: Eliot, Hemingway, Faulkner*. Nashville, TN: Vanderbilt University Press, 1971.

Weathers, Winston. *The Broken Word: The Communication Pathos in Modern Literature*. Communication and the Human Condition 1. Ed. Lee Thayer. New York: Gordon and Breach, 1981.

Weinstein, Mark A. "The Creative Imagination in Fiction and History." *Genre* 9 (1976): 263–77.

Weisenberger, Steven. Afterword to *Accident*. By Nicholas Mosley. Elmwood Park, IL: Dalkey Archive, 1966. 193–98.

West, Paul. *Sheer Fiction*. Kingston, NY: McPherson, 1988.

White, Hayden. *Metahistory: The Historical Imagination in Nineteenth-Century Europe*. Baltimore: Johns Hopkins University Press, 1973.

———. *Tropics of Discourse: Essays in Cultural Criticism*. Baltimore: Johns Hopkins University Press, 1978.

Whitehead, Alfred North. *Process and Reality*. New York: Macmillan, 1957.

Wilde, Alan. *Horizons of Assent: Modernism, Postmodernism, and the Ironic Imagina-*

tion. Baltimore: Johns Hopkins University Press, 1981; Philadelphia: University of Pennsylvania Press, 1987.

———. *Middle Grounds: Studies in Contemporary American Fiction*. Philadelphia: University of Pennsylvania Press, 1987.

———. " 'Strange Displacements of the Ordinary': Apple, Elkin, Barthelme, and the Problem of the Excluded Middle." *Boundary 2* 10 (Winter 1982): 177–99.

Wildman, Eugene. *Nuclear Love*. Athens: Ohio University Press, 1972.

Williams, William Carlos. *Imaginations*. New York: New Directions, 1970.

———. *Selected Essays*. New York: New Directions, 1954.

Wittgenstein, Ludwig. *Philosophical Grammar*. Ed. Rush Rhees. Trans. Anthony Kenny. Berkeley: University of California Press, 1974.

Woolf, Virginia. *To the Lighthouse*. New York: Harcourt Brace, 1927.

Wopitka, Paul. "Walter Abish's *How German Is It:* Representing the Postmodern." *Contemporary Literature* 30 (1989): 503–17.

Wordsworth, William. "The Tables Turned." *The Poetical Works of William Wordsworth*. Ed. E. DeSelincourt. London: Oxford University Press, 1920. 481.

Wurlitzer, Rudolph, *Flats*. New York: Dutton, 1970.

———. *Nog*. New York: Random, 1969.

Zavarzadeh, Mas'ud. *The Mythopoeic Reality: The Postwar American Nonfiction Novel*. Urbana: University of Illinois Press, 1976.

Index

PENN STUDIES IN CONTEMPORARY AMERICAN FICTION

A Series Edited by Emory Elliott, University of California at Riverside

Alan Wilde, *Middle Grounds: Studies in Contemporary American Fiction.*
1987

Brian Stonehill, *The Self-Conscious Novel: Artifice in Fiction from Joyce to Pynchon.* 1988

Silvio Gaggi, *Modern/Postmodern: A Study in Twentieth-Century Arts and Ideas.* 1989

John Johnston, *Carnival of Repetition: Gaddis's* The Recognitions *and Postmodern Theory.* 1990

Ellen Pifer, *Saul Bellow Against the Grain.* 1990

Arthur M. Saltzman, *Designs of Darkness in Contemporary American Fiction.* 1990

This book has been set in Linotron Galliard. Galliard was designed for Merganthaler in 1978 by Matthew Carter. Galliard retains many of the features of a sixteenth century typeface cut by Robert Granjon but has some modifications which give it a more contemporary look.

Printed on acid-free paper.